PARIS

PARIS
BETWEEN THE WARS

CAROL MANN

THE VENDOME PRESS

POUR ALICE ET RAPHAEL, MES PETITS PARISIENS

WITH THANKS TO MIKE DILLON ESPECIALLY AND ALEXANDRE VASSILIEV

First North American Edition

Published in the USA in 1996 by
The Vendome Press
1370 Avenue of the Americas
New York, NY 10019

Distributed in the USA and Canada by
Rizzoli International Publications
through St. Martin's Press
175 Fifth Avenue
New York, NY 10010

This book was designed and produced by
Calmann & King Ltd, London

Library of Congress Cataloging-in-Publication Data
Mann, Carol.
Paris between the wars: artistic life in the twenties and thirties / by Carol Mann.
p. cm
ISBN 0-86565-981-8
1. Paris (France)—Intellectual life—20th century. 2. Paris (France)—Social life and customs.
3. Arts—France—Paris—History—20th century. 4. Intellectuals—Homes and haunts—France—Paris. I. Title.
DC715.M34 1996
306.4'7'094436—dc20   96-18031
CIP

Designed by David Fordham
Picture research by Sue Bolsom-Morris

Printed and bound in Spain

Frontispiece:
Perfume shop of Richard Hudnut in the Rue de la Paix, c. 1928.
(photo: Thérèse Bonney)

CONTENTS

Direction CARMEN VILDEZ
LE COMIQUE
BRUEL
Sne VALROGER
LYMA
ROGER
LYMA
DIMANCHES
TOUS LES

INTRODUCTION

"LES ANNÉES FOLLES"

Paris has become simply awful — a kind of earthquake of motor cars, buses, trams, lorries, taxis and other howling and swooping and colliding engines . . . .
Edith Wharton

Paris in the twenties and thirties was the centre of Western literature, fine arts, architecture, design and fashion. The Ville Lumière, the City of Lights, drew and absorbed every aspect of creativity in one of the most exciting periods of this century. In a few years, the city went from post-war euphoria to prewar angst, from a shaky armistice to an unprecedented cataclysm. In those anxious and frenetic times, artists, poets and designers attempted to extract a semblance of meaning from their epoch, and in the process Paris absorbed the most sublime and abject aspects of the century.

Whatever may have been written about the so-called *années folles* ('crazy years'), the most striking aspect of the years following the armistice must have been the number of maimed soldiers on the Parisian sidewalks, and the cohorts of widows and orphans in black veils. They weren't the ones dancing the Charleston in beaded dresses in the nightclubs on the Left Bank. During the war a thousand young Frenchmen had been killed every day, at least twice that amount severely wounded, leaving everyone else, male

Street scene near the end of the Great War (*opposite*). By this time patriotism was wearing thin and it was increasingly difficult to work up enthusiasm for the wholesale slaughter going on in the battle-field. The streets were filled with maimed soldiers and cohorts of widows and orphans in black veils, a memory that was to haunt the interwar years and promote pacifism, even in the face of rising fascism.

Procession marking the end of the Great War, 1919 (*right*). Orphans parade in order to display their gratitude to the Americans for their intervention, despite the obvious mistake on the banner ('to' instead of 'from'). There were innumerable victory parades in every European capital, prominently featuring wounded soldiers and orphans.

and female, in a state of shock for years to come. This goes a long way to explaining some of the more extreme art manifestations of those two decades. Most Dada artists and Surrealist poets had either seen death on the front line or borne its gruelling consequences in freezing war-time Paris. Women, with financial burdens and responsibilities thrust upon them, found themselves tending traumatized invalids. Perhaps some of the short skirts and low pumps so typical of the period merely enabled them to deal with these new hardships. Life was indeed difficult in the Twenties. Prices shot up, and as the influence of the Russian revolution growled eastwards, strike followed strike and there was resentment against a society that had allowed such horrors to take place. Drastic measures were needed, not just to divert unpatriotic ire but to create employment, or at least a semblance of prosperity, to give meaning to such a hollow victory.

According to the Treaty of Versailles of 1919, Germany was supposed to pay France colossal war indemnities. While waiting, the French government (borrowing from Britain and especially the United States) supplied generous advances to companies who could start investing and expanding American-style. They ploughed a substantial part of their profits back into business: the economy grew even faster than the rising demand for newfangled electrical consumer goods. By the late Twenties, prosperity and

STREET SCENE in central Paris, mid 1930s. A push-cart in front of the largest department store in Paris, La Samaritaine, which sported the slogan 'You find everything at La Samaritaine'. Increasing office-jobs for women in the centre of Paris introduced new shopping habits. Henceforth lunch-time browsing also included buying food from such carts for the evening meal, to be lugged back on the metro home at night. (PHOTO: NOËL LE BOYER)

PARIS street scene in the mid 1930s. The legendary elegance of the Thirties was visible at every street corner. Not everyone could afford Haute Couture or even ready-to-wear clothing on sale in the department stores, but women avidly read fashion magazines, replete with patterns and extraordinarily precise descriptions of the latest trends which an able couturier could easily make up. (PHOTO: NOËL LE BOYER)

self-confidence had significantly been recovered. That Germany would not pay its debts and that Europe would collapse was not foreseen or even imagined. In the meantime, engineers and entrepreneurs travelled back and forth by liner to the States, in order to admire first hand the benefits to industry of Taylorism as applied by Henry Ford. All attempted to organize work in what seemed the most rational, or at any rate most productive way. Assembly lines became the norm in the larger factories, each worker repeating the same simple task all day. It was an exhausting and frustrating life, even though the eight-hour day was voted in in 1919, and in 1936 the Popular Front ordained a yearly one month holiday with pay. These factors led to the simultaneous rise of consumerism and revolutionary ideology left and right: the sheer anger and boredom provided suitable pent-up emotional motivation for both.

A large foreign work force – some two million workers – was imported: Peugeot, Citroën and Renault desperately needed manpower. Whereas before the war, immigrants had mainly come from Italy, Spain and Belgium, now Russia and Eastern Europe provided the main contingents, especially in the cities. From the Middle-East came Turks, and after the genocide of 1915, the first waves of Armenians. Integration was much more difficult and there seems to have been reticence on all sides. Nevertheless, Paris

CASINO DE PARIS, November 1938. A scene from the review *Amours de Paris*, the cast of over 300 artists included Maurice Chevalier.

INTERIOR of the Folies Bergère, 1928 (*opposite*). The eclectic Twenties at its wildest. Basically an adaptation of Greek-Roman atrium topped by a mould-cast glass cupola, a technique perfected by Lalique. The blousy flowers by Picot somehow jar with the Aztec style carpet, not enhanced by the furniture or the coloured marble columns. The patrons, however, must have been delighted by the profusion of decorative detail.

(PHOTO: SEEBERGER FRÈRES)

turned into the most cosmopolitan of European cities: restaurants, shops, and cafés sprang up to cater for all the different ethnic groups. It was also the most expensive city in Europe with low standards of modern comfort, since gas and electricity were exorbitant. Modernism, as before the war, was an aesthetic pioneered by artists and designers and only occasionally acted out by the wealthy and adventurous. Investors and planners soon turned over-cautious. In fact, it was in America that transplanted French *savoir-faire* was at its most influential. Parisian designers and stylists gave Hollywood silent movies their Art Deco dream dimension: Paul Iribe, followed by Erté, Maurice Leloir, René Hubert and most of the famous couturiers all went to Hollywood as if Parisian chic would give American movies that *je ne sais quoi* of true glamour.

Technology drove the post-war economies of the Western world (with the possible exception of Britain, which traditionally boosted economy with building). Conservative opposition to this was largely sentimental and nostalgic, coming from politicians who were trying to simultaneously promote a return to peasant (i.e. non-foreign) values and more restricted productivity. After all, one third of the population still lived *au village*. The increasing movement towards cities, especially Paris, made traditional luxury goods even more scarce: there were less peasants to seek truffles or

the chestnuts for *marrons glacés*. Those who migrated into cities brought their values with them, as did the hard headed fashion designer Coco Chanel who came from a grindingly poor peasant background. Peasant thrift, brimming with a suspicion against banking and investment, strongly permeated French economic thinking. Coupled with a deep-seated xenophobia, the result was a country that brought Pétain to power and became, by 1942, the most efficient Nazi colony in Europe.

A WEIGHT-LIFTER performing in the street in the mid-1930s (*above*). Wholesale unemployment obliged many people to invent new sources of income, so such street entertainment was frequent. This weight-lifter is probably a war-veteran.
(PHOTO: NOËL LE BOYER)

*S*UR LA TOUR EIFFEL, 1939 (*opposite*). This fashion shot caused a sensation when it appeared, as the model was strapped to the Eiffel Tower in a silk dress by Lucien Lelong. The courageous girl was Lisa Fonssagrives. The style is typical late Thirties neo-Victorian, complete with Balmoral-inspired tartan, reflecting the reactionary way in which women were perceived at the time. The photograph is by Erwin Blumenfeld (1897-1969), who went to Paris from Germany in 1936 and began working for French *Vogue* in 1938.

I
MYTHICAL
PARIS

I HAVE ONE COUNTRY- America is my country but Paris is my home town.

GERTRUDE STEIN

'PARIS IS REALLY A TEST for an American. Dinners, soirées, poets, erratic millionaires, painters, translations, lobsters, absinthe, music, promenades, oysters, sherry, aspirins, pictures, Sapphic heiresses, editors, books, sailors and how!' So the American poet Hart Crane described Paris in 1921. It certainly sums up what many immigrants saw in Paris, especially those who chose the Bohemian experience on the Left Bank of Paris. Part of its attraction, at least to poor Americans was the sheer cheapness of life. The franc fell steadily against the dollar after the war and extravagance was possible at last, at least until the Wall Street Crash in October 1929, which sunk many an American fortune being squandered in Paris.

In the early Twenties Montparnasse was the cultural hub of Paris, artists huddling in sidewalk cafés over a single *café creme* that lasted for hours. The owner of La Rotonde gave strict orders that none of them should ever be evicted. The hitherto calm, nearly rural neighbourhood began to change at a most frenetic pace, whilst the rest of Paris continued unperturbed. As the American poet e.e. cummings living in a hovel further down on the Rue Saint-André des Arts noted: 'The cathedral of Notre-Dame does not budge an inch for all the idiocies of this world.' Cafés, bars, *dancings* (dance halls) hotels and restaurants opened daily and the last stables in the neighbourhood were being rapidly converted into artists' studios. Artists, dancers and fugitives of every kind congregated on the miraculous Boulevard Montparnasse, between the Dome on its south side and the Rotonde on the north.

Some artists could afford to rent or even have studios built by famous architects: the Dadaist Tristan Tzara commissioned the Austrian architect Adolf Loos to build him a villa, the Russian émigrée sculptor Chana Orloff had Auguste Perret construct her a studio. But most artists lived in seedy hotels and relied on whatever additional floor-space the hotel manager could rent them as work premises. The American-born artist Man Ray, in the throes of a passionate affair with the model Kiki (by now the classic muse of the 14th *arrondissement*), invented rayographs in the Hotel des Ecoles

KIKI DE MONTPARNASSE, 1927. This legendary artists' model, who came to incarnate Montparnasse, was especially popular with the School of Paris. She posed for many paintings by Kisling, Othon Friesz and Foujita and had a tumultuous affair with Man Ray in whose work she also appears. In the mid-Twenties, she sang *risqué* songs in her own Montparnasse cabaret, L'Oasis, soon to be known as Chez Kiki. When she died in 1953, every Montparnasse café sent a wreath with their name inscribed on a purple ribbon, but Foujita and Oscar Dominguez were the only artists to attend her funeral. (PHOTO: ANDRÉ KERTESZ)

THE WRITER and collector Gertrude Stein (1874-1946) in her apartment at 27 Rue de Fleurus, with the American composer Virgil Thomson, c.1927-8 (*left*). Stein's most quoted (and probably her only remembered) sentence was: 'a rose is a rose is a rose', her own parallel to Cubism which she understood and admired. She was among the first, with her brother Leo, to collect and encourage both Picasso and Matisse. Among others, Thomson wrote the music for her opera, 'Four Saints in Three Acts' (1927-8), which was not produced until 1933, in America. (PHOTO: THÉRÈSE BONNEY)

in the Rue Delambre, round the corner from Le Dome and next to the American Dingo Bar, which sold corned beef sandwiches. He left the contents of his pockets, bits of string, crumpled paper and cotton wool on photosensitive paper placed on the dusty floor by an open window with legendary results. In the late Twenties, he had become such a success that he could afford two studios, one south of the Boulevard Montparnasse in the Rue Campagne-Première, and the other opposite the Luxembourg gardens.

In the early Thirties, though foreigners represented under ten per cent of the total population, they accounted for at least half of the artists in Paris, possibly much more in Montparnasse. For example, while the writers and thinkers of the Surrealist movement, André Breton, Philippe Soupault, Paul Eluard and Louis Aragon were French, in typical Parisian fashion many of the artists came from all over the world: Max Ernst and Hans Bellmer were German, Joan Miró, Luis Buñuel and Salvador Dalí Spanish, and René Magritte Belgian. Art in the inter-war years was Parisian in its unique cosmopolitan expression.

Most of the artists of the School of Paris lived in Montparnasse, a number of whom (for example, the painters Tsugoharu Foujita, Moïse Kisling, Diego Rivera, Chaim Soutine and Pinchus Kremègne, and the sculptors Constantin Brancusi, Jacques Lipchitz, Ossip Zadkine and Chana

SYLVIA BEACH (1887-1962), American editor and bookshop operator, c.1925/30 (*opposite*). In the Twenties her shop and lending library 'Shakespeare and Company', founded in 1919, was a gathering place for Anglo-Saxon expatriate writers as well as for French authors discovering their interest for the USA. In 1922 she published James Joyce's *Ulysses* after it had been refused by many outraged publishers and generously allowed him unlimited corrections of his proofs.

*K*ANDINSKY in December 1936. The Russian born Wassily Kandinsky (1866-1944) was already an elderly artist when, after the Bauhaus had been closed down by the Nazis, he fled Hitler's Germany to come to France in 1933. A pioneer of abstract art, his work in France was only appreciated by a knowledgeable and limited avant-garde and he felt isolated from current trends. He is shown here in the studio Duchamp found for him in Neuilly.

Orloff) had arrived in Paris before the war. Many were Jews from Eastern Europe, simultaneously fleeing anti-semitism, and the restrictive life in the *shtetl* where a career as an artist was unthinkable. Unlike the Americans, these Jewish artists were mainly poor and really survived through solidarity with members of their own group, helping newcomers adapt themselves to the city of their wildest dreams. Not all stayed. Marc Chagall had gone back to Russia to join the revolution only to return with Bella and their son in 1923. The painter Amedeo Modigliani, a Sephardi Jew from Livorno and Soutine's hero, had died in abject misery in the early days of 1920. Others joined the area, where artists reigned on the boulevard and countless parties took place, night after night. This was the single focal point of the universe, even the purist painter Piet Mondrian was part of the fun, having lived in Montparnasse before the war and returned there after it. In 1926, when Holland forbade the practice of the Charleston on grounds of obscenity, he officially told a Dutch journalist that he would never return to his homeland, devoted as he was to the Charleston, and, as the journalist noted, he practised religiously at home every Sunday with gramophone records.

For many liberal expatriates from Central and Eastern Europe, Paris stood for freedom and still embodied the values of the French Revolution. The tens of thousands of Germans fleeing Hitler from 1933 onwards (including the Russian painter Wassily Kandinsky) came to what they considered the very cradle of democracy. For the Russian aristocracy, whose mother tongue was French, fleeing Lenin then Stalin, France represented the exact opposite: the old world of lost gentility and courtly privileges. The reality was, of course, neither and many foreign immigrants soon found France less enlightened than they had expected. In particular, the reaction against Jewish artists grew virulently throughout the Twenties to the extent that the very term 'School of Paris' came to be synonymous with the work of foreign, Jewish artists and was contrasted with that of the 'French School' of native artists. Accusations were made by critics that the French tradition had been corrupted by this influx of foreigners, and a host of other national ailments came to be laid at the door of the Jews by right-wing figures.

Some of the Russian immigrants had to work for the first time in their lives. The Boulogne Renault factories provided employment for many members of the Russian and Cossack military. The nobility and wealthy bourgeoisie from Russia became taxi-drivers, having been privileged enough to own motor cars in Saint Petersburg before the revolution: in the inter-war years, half of the taxis in Paris were driven by Russians. Their wives and daughters became piano teachers and governesses. Many a forlorn Russian princess spent her first years in Paris in some dingy hotel room, sewing, embroidering or threading beads for the elaborate evening dresses in fashion. Sonia Terk and Princess Youssoupoff did manage to benefit from this experience: Sonia became a well known artist, marrying the painter Robert Delaunay, and Irina opened a renowned couture house called Irfé (Irina + Felix), with her husband Felix famous for having assassinated Rasputin. Other immigrants launched leading fashion magazines like *Jardin des Modes*, *Harper's Bazaar* and *Vogue*. A number of noble émigrées became much sought-after models, working for leading couturiers, their famished slenderness envied by overweight Parisiennes: the most famous one must be Natalie Paley, daughter of Grand Duke Paul, who married the couturier Lucien Lelong and became one of the most elegant beauties of the Thirties.

For Americans like the writers Ernest Hemingway, Ezra Pound, e.e. cummings and Janet Flanner (who became Paris correspondent for *The New Yorker*), Paris represented an escape from a conservative rather stuffy world

excruciatingly devoid of real art, something Gertrude Stein, the doyenne of American émigrés had known since 1903. In the Twenties, litres of wine, pastis, cognac, marc, calvados, absinthe (still available in some places) helped to wash down the strain Prohibition had put on them at home. Many of the Allied soldiers had perceived something of the potential excitement of 'Paree' during the war. They probably idealized these memories as they returned home, especially as this would have been their first glimpse of civilian pleasures after the appalling years in the trenches.

As the literary, as well as artistic, capital of the West, Paris was home to a panoply of native talent, including Marcel Proust (who died in 1922), and also attracted many writers from abroad. In 1919 the American Sylvia Beach opened 'Shakespeare and Company', a publishing house and lending library to which Gertrude Stein, André Gide, Jules Romains and, in 1935, the student Simone de Beauvoir all subscribed. She published James Joyce's *Ulysses* in 1922, whereupon a disgusted Stein cancelled her subscription. American musicians also crowded Paris: George Gershwin wrote his 'An American in Paris' in a Right Bank hotel in 1928. His friend Cole Porter lived just north of Montparnasse for the entire inter-war period, in a flat covered in zebra skins. The jazz age was distinctly Parisian. One of the

*B*ASTILLE DAY, 14 July 1934. The street ball on the 14th of July - more precisely on the night of the 13/14 July - was the most popular outdoor ball and was usually organized by the firemen of each *arrondissement* to celebrate the taking of the Bastille which inaugurated the French Revolution. Dancing here has carried on through the day, with the atmosphere Jean Rhys wrote about at the time (*Good Morning Midnight*): 'The streets blazing hot and eating peaches. The long lovely blue days that lasted for ever, that still are'.

*W*AITERS race across Montmartre on 8 March 1935. An annual contest that still takes place in Paris, where waiters in full uniform have to run through their *arrondissement*, impeccably holding a tray with a bottle and two glasses. This press photograph has been retouched, and the faces of the waiters have been highlighted in white, a typical procedure at the time.

outstanding figures of the period was the heiress Nancy Cunard, famous in Man Ray portraits wearing the enormous African bangles given to her by her then lover Aragon.

It was not only émigrés and visitors who romanticized Paris: the Surrealists, for example, felt the city central to their experience of life and recorded accounts of their aimless wanderings in search of chance and unusual events. Aragon's *Paris Peasant* (1926) is full of odd observations and associative thoughts, spurred by his strolls around the Passage de l'Opéra ('a big glass coffin') and the Buttes de Chaumont. In his book *Nadja* (1928) Breton describes his strange encounter with the alluring woman of the title, mixing this with impressions and anecdotes about the city, which he thought one of only two in France where 'something worth while' could happen to him. The city provided relentless inspiration. The American writer, Henry Miller, who returned to live in Paris in 1930, felt this was the only place an artist could live with dignity: 'The streets sing, the stones talk. The houses drip history, glory and romance'.

CAFÉ SCENE in Montparnasse, c.1930. The art works that decorate the premises may have been left on the premises in lieu of payment as was frequent at the time. Aicha, the famous black model, is seated in the foreground. She posed for most of the School of Paris. Legend has it that before the First World War Lenin took to modelling for artists as well, and as he was always short of cash, generous Aicha frequently helped him out, something she was to do for a great number of down and out artists on the boulevard throughout her tumultous life.

*L*A ROTONDE, 105 Boulevard Montparnasse (*above*). The café had been run since 1911 by Victor Libion, who made it a haven for painters, poets and writers of all nationalities, allowing them to linger over a single *café-crème* for hours. Like many other Montparnasse café and restaurant owners he amassed a considerable collection of art-works given in lieu of payment.

*F*ANCY DRESS BALL on the theme of 'Antiquity during the reign of Louis XIV' (*left*), a party given by the art patron Count Etienne de Beaumont in the garden of his splendid *hôtel particulier*, the Hôtel Masseran on the 30 May 1923. Darius Milhaud in a curly Louis XIV wig stands by Georges Auric.

*I*NTERIOR of La Coupole, 102 Boulevard du Montparnasse, c.1930. Opened in 1927, this café and restaurant rapidly became emblematic of Montparnasse. For the legendary launching party on an icy night in December 1927 over three thousand invitations were issued and about two thousand bottles of champagne were consumed by the most famous artists of the day and their gatecrashing friends, most of whom had to be forcibly removed by the police at five o'clock the next morning.

*T*HE CAFÉ DU DÔME, 108 Boulevard du Montparnasse, 1920s (*above*). A group of American artists and musicians. This café on the south side of the Boulevard Montparnasse opposite La Rotonde was a daytime American stronghold whereas Le Select two doors down was particularly favoured by Hemingway and Miller after dusk because whisky was served all night. When they got too nostalgic, the 'Parisites', as young Americans were referred to by exasperated locals, crossed the road to The Jockey, which opened in 1923 and where the American owner Hilaire Hiler had attempted to recreate a typical cowboy saloon. (PHOTO: THÉRÈSE BONNEY)

THE ARTIST and costume designer Valentine Hugo at the Ball of Count de Beaumont, c.1925 (*opposite, below*). The indomitable Valentine in some theatrical performance at one of the marvellous fancy-dress ball which gave the *Années Folles* their wild reputation. This one was given by that most elegant patron of the arts, Count Etienne de Beaumont.

PARTY held in Montparnasse on the occasion of the Futurist exhibition at Galerie 23 in December 1929 (*above*). The inauguration of the exhibition included a Futurist concert of music by Luigi Russolo. Futurism, as expounded by its founder the Italian poet Tommaso Marinetti in 1909 was the precursor to Dada in its destruction of conventional art in favour of an aesthetic based on machines and speed. Though it continued after the war, by then it had lost its innovative, anarchic energy. (PHOTO: ANDRÉ KERTESZ)

*P*ARC DES BUTTES CHAUMONT in the mid 1930s. A popular landscaped park which dominated the north of Paris, it was the scene of many Sunday afternoon family outings. It was also one of the subjects of Aragon's musings in *Paris Peasant* (1926) after a visit there with Breton and Marcel Noll: 'We enter the park feeling like conquerors and quite drunk with open-mindedness'.
(PHOTO: LOUIS CAILLAUD)

SKATING in the Bois de Vincennes, 1929. The Bois de Vincennes (later the site of the 1931 Colonial Exhibition) in the East of Paris was the place where most Eastern and Central European Jewish immigrants went to relax, as it was the park nearest to the central areas of Paris (including the Sentier and the Marais where they lived and worked in the rag trade). (PHOTO: LOUIS CAILLAUD)

A STEAM MERRY-GO ROUND (*overleaf*). In nearly every quarter, there was a merry-go-round usually dating from the turn of the century like this one, much to the delight of the children and their dizzy parents. (PHOTO: DONALD McLEISH)

29

A GROUP of Russian émigrés at the house of Ilka and Eva Révai, 1927 (*above*). After the Revolution, Russians came over to Paris in waves, having idealized the city since the nursery, where many of them spoke French. Ilka was a photographer and his wife Eva did embroidery, like so many émigrées. The handicrafts that genteel young girls learnt as children helped them survive, especially in the Twenties, when beads, tassels and embroidered motifs were all the rage. (PHOTO: ANDRÉ KERTESZ)

T SUGOHARU FOUJITA (1886-1968) and his wife Youki, c.1927 (*opposite*). Born in Japan, Foujita sailed to France in 1913. After years of poverty, he shot to fame in the Twenties, painting cats, nudes and society ladies in a diluted Japanese manner. Around 1926, with Youki, he left Montparnasse for the conventionally elegant 16th *arrondissement*, where he gave dazzling parties until the taxes caught up with him with in 1929, making them near penniless. In the Thirties Youki became the partner of the Surrealist poet Robert Desnos.

*T*HE DUTCH ARTIST Piet Mondrian (1872-1944) in his studio at 26 Rue du Départ, next to the Montparnasse railway station, in 1926 (*above*). Mondrian was the pioneer of that most austere form of abstract painting, Neo-Plasticism, which used only the primary colours red, blue and yellow in a rigid black grid. His studio was decorated in the same severe style and some of the coloured rectangles that adorned it can be seen on the walls behind him. (PHOTO: ANDRÉ KERTESZ)

*T*HE SCULPTOR Jacques Lipchitz (1891-1973) in 1935 (*opposite*). Born in Lithuania, he moved to Paris in 1913, where he quickly evolved a Cubist style. Like so many artists of the School of Paris he had lived in poverty in Montparnasse, though by the time this photograph was taken he had become successful. (PHOTO: ANDRÉ ROGI)

THE SCULPTRESS Chana Orloff (1888-1968), with her son Elie, in her studio, c.1924. Born in the Ukraine, she moved to Paris in 1910 where she remained until her death. Displayed around her are a number of her sculptures, including *Maternity* (1924) on the left. Her work drew on the modern styles of the period, such as Cubism, but remained essentially traditional. She later commissioned a modernist studio (1926) from Auguste Perret. (PHOTO: THÉRÈSE BONNEY)

*K*ISLING with an unknown model. All his life Kisling painted plump doll-like figures that
have come to characterize not only the School of Paris, but the more decorative painterly
Twenties. The famed Kiki de Montparnasse was his favourite model and her curves
served to counteract the emaciated boyish figures so much in vogue in fashion drawings.

MADAME PAUL DUBONNET posing in the studio of the Dutch artist Kees van Dongen (1877-1968). This is a far cry from the days when van Dongen, as a young artist living in the Bateau-Lavoir, contributed satirical drawings to the magazine *Assiette au Beurre* at the turn of the century. By now he was rich and successful, famous for an opulent life style and endless parties, like Foujita. Here he paints the wife of the president of the Dubonnet company in a predictable setting of gold *lamé* and furs.
(PHOTO: THÉRÈSE BONNEY)

MARC CHAGALL (1887-1985) in front of his painting *Solitude* in 1934 (*above*). Born in Vitebsk, in 1923 he returned to Paris where he had already lived in utter misery from 1910 to 1914. In the meantime he lost some 150 canvases which he had left in his studio in 'La Ruche' before his departure. Henceforth, he was never to be financially worried again. At the time this photograph was taken, he was increasingly alarmed by the development of fascism all over Europe. As a Jewish artist, especially one who used overtly Jewish iconography in his work, he felt particularly vulnerable.

TAMARA DE LEMPICKA (1898-1980) in 1928 (*opposite*). Shown at home painting the unfinished portrait of her then husband, Tadeusz de Lempicki (who she divorced at this time). She was a Pole with a Saint Petersburg education who arrived in Paris in 1918 and was a pupil of the Cubist André Lhote. Her highly distinctive, decorative works have a sleekness typical of the period. The following year she had a studio built for her by Mallet-Stevens.
(PHOTO: THÉRÈSE BONNEY)

*L*E MONOCLE, a notorious lesbian club in Montparnasse which ran from 1935 to 1940.

A NTOINE PEVSNER in his studio, c.1938. Antoine Pevsner (1886-1962) was the brother of the sculptor Naum Gabo. He was born in Kiev and twice lived in Paris (1911 and 1913) before 1917 when he returned to Russia following the Revolution. There he worked with Tatlin and Malevich, but returned to Paris in 1923 when the official Soviet attitude to abstract art made his life and career unlivable there.
(PHOTO: DENISE BELLON)

*T*HE STUDIO of Moïse Kisling (1891-1953) in 1938. This shows his wall of photographs of friends (including himself, on the right, and Cocteau), film stars and models. Also included are various other artists of the motley group called the School of Paris. Poignantly, two of the photographs (both near the centre) are of artists long dead: Amedeo Modigliani, who had died in 1920, and Jules Pascin, who had committed suicide in 1930. By this date the Bohemian days of the Twenties must have seemed far off. (PHOTO: DENISE BELLON)

2
STREET LIFE

You enter by accident in the Grand Café
Dazzled by the boulevard lights
Comfortably seated in front of the large table
You drank with an unquenchable thirst
Beautiful made-up faces wished you bonsoir
CHARLES TRENET: *Le Grand Café* (1937)

IN THE TWENTIES AND THIRTIES, the street turned into the sparkling theatre of modern life. Urban mass culture began to supersede and replace traditional popular culture, which had hitherto been based on peasant ritual and prescribed religious holidays. After the war, a revolutionary idea emerged: fun was something anybody could buy all year round. One of the first laws the government voted in was the eight hour day (1919), and the new-found consumer society put leisure on sale on every street corner where movie-theatres, cabarets and department stores flourished.

For the first time in history, working people had time they could really call their own, something their own parents could not have imagined in their most hedonistic dreams. It was customary to read a morning and an evening paper, so that everyone felt themselves concerned by the tumultuous changes that were sweeping the globe. *Le Petit Parisien, Le Petit Journal, Le Journal, Le Matin* and *L'Echo de Paris* kept the Parisians abreast of the news. There were scandals galore – from Isadora Duncan's latest tragedy, to the murderer Landru's most recent female victim, not forgetting the all-important sports page. From the early Twenties onwards, the radio provided a welcome if frequently scrambled and blurred addition to the home, and listening to the post-prandial news turned into the most solemn of family rituals. In Germany, Goebbels, the propaganda minister of the Reich was prompt in putting this medium to full use.

It was not only the wealthy who went out. Cabarets, night-clubs, popular theatre and cinema were geared to a working- and middle-class audience for whom entertainment was an excursion into an improbably luxurious world. Theatre was still extremely popular with those who could afford the trimmings, as half the fun was the dressing-up, the long intermission at the bar and the *souper* afterwards in some extravagant dive. However, Paris was

THE DANCERS Colette Roby (niece of Colette) and Suzanne Blanchet in their shrimp costumes for *Trois Filles Nues* at the Bouffes-Parisiennes, c.1925.

not Berlin or Moscow, and truly experimental theatre could not flourish on the complacent bourgeois stage. Comedy was in, not the farcical pre-war genre, but the cynical plays about modern life, especially the thrills of adultery. In the Thirties, references to contemporary politics were sought, as if some meaning to that troubled epoch could be found through handy stage aphorisms. Hence the success of Jean Giraudoux, especially his *La Guerre de Troie n'aura pas lieu* ('The Trojan War Will not Take Place', 1935), which opened just as Mussolini was pounding his way through Ethiopia. A few intimate and surreal dramas were also performed for the benefit of a handful of would-be decadent intellectuals, whilst everyone else packed into the boulevard cafés, ran to the Folies Bergère, Bobino and L'Olympia, not to mention the lesser cabarets and night-clubs, eager to laugh, be dazzled and forget the tough post-war realities outside the plush and gilt theatres. Art galleries, fashionable boutiques and international exhibitions all provided entertainment, as long as whatever on show remained decorative, teasingly provocative even, but not intellectually challenging.

In the Twenties, designers like Paul Poiret at the Casino de Paris and Erté at the Folies Bergère created costumes of such lavishness (and expense) that much of Parisian night-life was endowed with mythical splendour. Russian-born Erté, described by *Harper's Bazaar* as the 'World's Foremost Fashion

JOSEPHINE BAKER at the *Fête des Caf' Conc*, 1926. Baker typified the stereotype of the black burlesque figure, which made her sensuousness on stage acceptable in a way the white equivalent would have been censored. It would have been hard to imagine Mistinguett getting away with a comparable role in anything more than an intimate setting. Apart from a few extremely isolated nightclubs, jazz was played by white musicians in dress suits.

SAINTE CATHERINE at Paul Poiret's, 25 November 1925. Paul Poiret gave Josephine Baker (seated in the centre) free clothes in exchange for publicity for his fading business. With La Revue Nègre, Baker had just brought the jazz age to Paris, complete with banana belts, camouflage feathers, steamy plumage and post-tribal sensuousness.

Genius' also designed marvellous costumes for Hollywood. French intervention was to save the famous black performer Josephine Baker. The legendary Revue Nègre, brought from America to Paris by Rolf de Maré, started as a rather dowdy spectacle at the Théâtre des Champs Elysées in September 1925. The whole enterprise would have been doomed without Parisian *savoir-faire* as a result of which carnival costumes, fancy décor and a more innovative choreography were introduced. When Josephine Baker was asked to appear naked but for some strategic foliage, in true French cabaret style, she threatened to return to the States immediately. Jacques-Charles, the designer, pleaded with her to take her final decision after the première, and the success was such that Baker stayed on for the rest of her life, moving on to become the undisputed star of the Folies Bergère. Banana belts, camouflage feathers, steamy plumage, post-tribal sensuousness, the jazz age *à la parisienne* had come to town: the Parisians lapped it all up and chorused for more. But black music was nevertheless played by white musicians in dress suit.

Despite the real hatred reactionaries bore against what they viewed as a Transatlantic threat to French civilisation from jazz, the blackbottom and the Charleston, the *américain* label conferred indubitable modernity on just about anything, especially cocktails like the smooth *americano*, a vermouth served in the *bar américain* of La Coupole. Nightclubs in Montparnasse like La Jungle, which opened in 1927 and had become all the rage by the following year, had a pianist playing ragtime and blues: dancers, cheek to cheek, buttock to buttock, crowded the minuscule dance floor night after night. Across the road, Kiki the model was entertaining her crowd at The Jockey, a small nightclub that ran from 1923 to 1930. Flaunting her by now legendary charms, she sang *canaille* songs full of naughty double-entendre.

In Montmartre, you could still experience some of Toulouse-Lautrec's excitement in front of genuine Can-Can as performed in the Bal Tabarin. The Moulin Rouge had, however, burnt down in 1914 and with it the most famous music-hall of the Belle Epoque. Gone were the days of lute-strumming courtesans and scatological crudities, to be replaced by the all-engulfing spectacle, be it a snappy review or the Blues Bars run by Americans, like the Bricktop patronized by Aragon and his Surrealist pals.

In the hard-up Thirties people could no longer afford lavish spectacles in their daily lives. The artifice and glitter of the stage was a far cry, even in the Twenties, from what was going on in the street. The costume designers in the theatre would have been unemployable in real life – Poiret was by then totally *passé*, while Chanel's sober, practical styles corresponded more to women's lives. Instead of yearly reviews, theatres would stage just one lavish spectacle over a period of three to four years. Even the *revues légères*, lightweight and *deshabillé*, weren't bringing in the crowds. The Concert Mayol, with such opulently erotic shows as *Nu . . . 1934* or *Nuits perverses* was close to bankruptcy, the décor and artistic absence of costumes proving too expensive. Tourists and visitors from the provinces would explore such places, eager for a peek at *bon ton* naughtiness, especially during the 1937 International Exhibition; they would then tour the nearby dubious pensions and bars for alternative entertainment at the price of ever growing venereal disease. Health authorities spoke of eight million syphilitics and casualties comparable to Verdun. The absence of legal contraception made life difficult, and Parisians, like everyone else in the Thirties, sought escape of the most imaginative kind – before the war caught up with them.

Parisians looked to the magic of the movies, which since the advent of the talkies in the late Twenties, was turning into mass entertainment. It offered even more of a fantasy world than the stage and was cheaper, so that the whole family could join in the frequently boisterous fun. People

*E*NRICO PRAMPOLINI with the actress Maria Ricotti, 1927. The Italian Futurist Prampolini was often in Paris between 1925 and 1937 and with Ricotti created a touring pantomime theatre, the Theatre of Futurist Pantomime. Its performance in Paris in 1927 was officially boycotted by the Surrealists in Paris but also travelled to America.
(PHOTO: THÉRÈSE BONNEY)

THEATRE
MADELEINE
DE LA
25 AVRIL
25 MAI
1927
THEATRE
THEATRE
DE LA
PANTOMIME
INTERPRETATION
MIMIQUE
MARIA
RICOTTI
DIRECTION ARTISTIQUE
E. PRAMPOLINI

generally went to the local film showing down the road: historical weepies and cynical dramas were particularly prized. Abel Gance's epic *Napoléon* (1927; replete with tricoteuses wearing their bonnets pulled down to their eyebrows in true *garçonne* fashion) provided priceless thrills that were easy to repeat at the next movie session. For those anxious to make up what they might have missed, they could read the *ciné-romans* (novelettes based on the film) on the tram to work. The period was beset by banking disasters and almost daily financial scandals, such as the Stavisky affair of 1934, and movies about successful criminals like *Avec le sourire* (1936) proved immensely appealing to a by now somewhat disillusioned public, convinced they were witnessing life as it really was. In this film Maurice Chevalier played a debonair crook gleefully causing the ruin of an honest man, reduced to the station of a beggar.

In the Thirties, cinema managers offered double bills plus a newsreel and cartoon, and the theatre proportionately suffered a decline. Nevertheless, the public still demanded its share of live entertainment and a great assortment of spectacles was available in Paris day and night. For the sake of show-business, a number of cabarets went back to variety shows, where singers, clowns and comedians would alternate in the same evening. At the Empire, Charles Trenet would croon, Captain Wall entertained with his

*C*INEMA CLUNY (*above, left*). In the interwar years, cinema became the most popular form of entertainment. Situated in the Latin Quarter, this movie-theatre would have showed more experimental films. The façade has an ancient, mysterious quality, reminiscent of Japanese temple architecture, which is set off by the modernistic lettering.
(PHOTO: THÉRÈSE BONNEY)

*T*HE FOLIES BERGÈRE during the erection of the new façade, c.1928 (*above, right*). The dancing figure in the centre panel is framed in the popular ziggurat style which even artists used to frame their pictures in galleries.
(PHOTO: THÉRÈSE BONNEY)

JEANNE BOURGEOIS, alias Mistinguett, on the staircase of the Moulin Rouge, 1925/6. The legendary Mistinguett (1873-1956) created reviews alongside Maurice Chevalier with hit songs to which all Paris sang along, especially when they were relayed on the radio in the evening. At well over fifty and at the height of her fame, a star in 'La revue de Mistinguett' and 'Ça c'est Paris', the plumed *étoile* and part-time *femme fatale* droned 'Mon Homme' while flaunting her seemingly immortal legs. But her ever-adoring Parisian public hardly batted a kohled eyelid. The photograph illustrates the typical disparity between sylph-like drawings and the less than photogenic reality.

(PHOTO: THÉRÈSE BONNEY)

performing crocodiles, Jack Hylton stomped along with his 'merrie' orchestra, and Barbette flung himself off his trapeze. But what really drew the crowds was *la chanson*. Singers were no longer asked to act (like Mistinguett at the Folies Bergère) or look decorative like Belle Epoque beauties, they merely had to sing something that people – women in particular – could relate to their real lives. Passion, jealousy, even murderous feelings, filled the songs. Viviane Romance, Lucienne Boyer and Damia sang their way into the hearts of France. Male singers too provided the stuff of dreams: the indomitable Maurice and Tino Rossi broke hearts the way the clown Bagessen had hitherto smashed plates on stage; Jean Sablon shocked everyone in 1936 by singing with a microphone he had brought back from America.

The other new source of entertainment was window shopping, especially on Saturday afternoons. Cafés, *salons de thé*, cocktail bars and brasseries

provided welcome watering holes between sessions on the crowded boulevards: Frenchmen drank more than anyone else in Europe, a couple of litres a day being the national average. And to this, you added the statutory *apéritif* and *digestif.* Leaving their men propped up in bars, the women fluttered in and out of the gorgeous boutiques and cut-price stores. Established firms opened cheap retail stores such as Prisunic and Monoprix. Here, shoppers could browse and day-dream before inexpensive, mass-produced wares in warm surroundings which increasingly attracted the idle and the unemployed looking to kill time pleasantly. Similar stores of the kind mushroomed all over the city even in the elegant Avenue de l'Opéra, provided one could wade through the steadily increasing traffic jams. In 1931, pedestrian crossings appeared followed by innocuous traffic lights activated by a gloved gendarme's hand. The City of Lights by now truly deserved its name, neon signs, theatrical street lighting, flashing car lights illuminated the Art Deco nights and walking across Paris provided continuous if precarious delight.

STREET MARKET in the mid 1930s. Each *arrondissement* (here the south side of the 18th) had several markets held on prescribed days of the week where it was customary to buy fresh food, meat and fish, rather than in specialized shops as in Britain or the USA.
(PHOTO: NOËL LE BOYER)

*F*ISHING by the Seine in the mid 1930s. Fishing along the Seine was frequent, not just from the islands but on each side of the river and fish abounded, despite the noise and pollution from the barges. (PHOTO: NOËL LE BOYER)

*T*HE SAMARITAINE BATHING-POOL on the Seine, 1926. Ever since the Twenties, any outdoor sports producing a lean, tanned body were in. Yet menswear etiquette still insisted on having a covered torso. As these bathing suits were knitted, they must have been far more revealing when wet.
(PHOTO: SEEBERGER FRÈRES)

*B*ASTILLE DAY, 14 July 1928 (*above*). Children join the fun in their Sunday best, short starched cotton frocks and long white socks that reveal rickets more often than not. Children's fashions of the interwar years have become classics: smocked dresses, T-bar shoes and tweed coats with velvet collars all originate from these years.

*S*AINTE CATHERINE, 25 November 1929 (*opposite, above*). Saint Catherine's feast day was an opportunity for unmarried working girls to have a field day, they were meant to indicate their state - over 25 and still available - by donning an elaborately amusing hat.

*R*EHEARSAL for the Gala de l'Union des Artistes at the Cirque d'Hiver, 110 Rue Amelot (11th *arrondissement*), with Maurice Chevalier, 28 February 1937 (*opposite, below*). This annual event took place on the 6 March. Maurice Chevalier was definitely a favourite among Paris crooners. There was nothing Parisians loved so much as a good *chanson* they could sing to. On the stage, on screen, here in the circus, a straw *canotier* in his hand, Maurice certainly got them humming, even with war looming large.

MARDI GRAS, 6 March 1935 (*above*). Local lads sport masks of leading politicians, including Hitler at furthest left and Léon Blum in front of him. Totalitarian regimes were coming to the fore, and Doumergue's government attempted contradictory compromises in order to keep the spectre of war away. In January 1935 France signed a treaty with Mussolini and in May, a mutual asssistance pact with Russia.

BAL DES QUAT'Z' ARTS, 25 June 1939 (*opposite*). This annual student ball was an occasion to dress up extravagantly and an excuse for the whole Latin Quarter to behave outrageously. The theme that year was the Sack of Byzantium and here art students, dressed as Byzantine and Moorish warriors, wield their cardboard sabres against the remnants of a Roman statue in the courtyard of the Ecole des Beaux-Arts.

*A*RTISTES AUTOMOBILE CHAMPIONSHIP, 8 May 1934 (*above*). On the left, Rose Lorraine dons the latest mermaid figure, complete with gauntlet and picture hat worn at the back of the head to display her forehead, contrary to Twenties fashion. Laure Diana, next to the famous boxer Georges Carpentier, deliberately resists Thirties feminisation. Her double breasted jacket and tie shows that she would be professionally successful in a male dominated work place.

*T*HE GARÇONNES, 1928 (*opposite*). These are characters in a film called *La Symphonie Pathétique*, with Madeleine Messayer, Michèle Verly and Olga Day. This was a rather adventurous film where the central hero appears in the style of Radcliffe Hall, the English lesbian author. (PHOTO: JACQUES-HENRI LARTIGUE)

*T*HE FRATELLINI CLOWNS, c.1931. From left to right, they are: François, Albert and Paul and their portraits appear on the caravan beside them. The Fratellini brothers were the star clowns at the Cirque Médrano in Montparnasse, which had been a popular haunt for many artists since before the war. They were also artistic directors of the Cirque d'Hiver and even appeared in Cocteau's *Le Boeuf sur le Toit*. Their performances were influenced by their artist friends - Calder, a great fan of the circus, used to make props for them, including a dog constructed from rubber tubing.
(PHOTO: THÉRÈSE BONNEY)

*S*ACHA GUITRY. The renowned actor during the filming of the outdoor shots of *Neuf Célibataires* ('Nine Bachelors') in the Rue Saint-Vincent, 18th *arrondissement*, on 16 June 1939. On stage and in films, he played just about the same role throughout his career, that of the urbane Parisian Don Juan relentlessly crushing forlorn bourgeois hearts. (PHOTO: ANDRÉ ZUCCA)

*B*ASTILLE DAY, 14 July 1930. Dancing overflowed from one café terrace to the next and onto the street. Note the formality of the men's dress at this time. The women wear cloche hats, dancing with seemingly irrepressible gaiety. Perhaps that is what Hemingway meant when he thought of Paris as 'a moveable feast'.

A DOUGHNUT stand in 1925 (*above*). An incredibly swish shop front for rather banal pastries ('Krapfen' is the German for doughnut) in a poor neighbourhood: 17 Rue de Lappe in the Bastille area. (PHOTO: SEEBERGER FRÈRES)

A DELIVERY TRUCK, c.1930 (*opposite, above*). The most avant-garde graphics invaded urban spaces, posters and wall paintings, and here appear on a delivery truck bearing the Monsavon soap logo designed by Jean Carlu. (PHOTO: THÉRÈSE BONNEY)

B OUTIQUE UNION DES FRANCS, c.1927 (*right*). Typical of the period, the shop retains the traditional façade, its modernity being asserted solely through the use of extremely dominant lettering. (PHOTO: THÉRÈSE BONNEY)

R ODY BAR, 1927 (*opposite, below*). The façade is by Jan and Joël Martel who have given the otherwise innocuous café a mono-lithic temple structure complete with monumental lettering. (PHOTO: THÉRÈSE BONNEY)

*F*ILLING STATION in 1925. In the days before traffic lights and white-gloved policemen (all of which appeared in the Thirties), cars were already taking over from horse-drawn carriages.
(PHOTO: SEEBERGER FRÈRES)

CHIQUITO NIGHT-CLUB, designed by Charles Siclis (*above*). A new Basque Bar, as can be seen in the extravagant wall decorations in the style of railway posters. The elaborate engraved glass is a curious mixture of Mondrian and Art Deco at its blousiest, contrasting, not altogether pleasantly, with the Thonet style bistro furniture.
(PHOTO: THÉRÈSE BONNEY)

LA PERRUCHE NIGHT-CLUB in Montmartre (*opposite*). The parrot is rendered in Aztec style in the most popular of Twenties colours, green. (PHOTO: THÉRÈSE BONNEY)

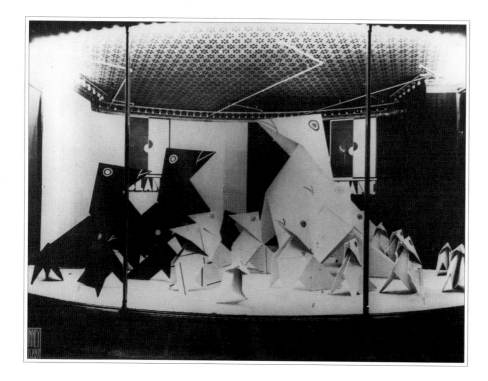

*B*OUTIQUE PIERRE IMANS, showing a display of mannequins, c.1928 (*above*). The window presents an ideal mix of Deauville and Saint Tropez. Beach holidays and tanning were all the rage in the slim Twenties.
(PHOTO: THÉRÈSE BONNEY)

*W*INDOW DISPLAY in the Galeries Lafayette during the 'white sale', 1927 (*left*). The traditional Japanese art of Origami lends itself beautifully to a Cubist interpretation, while the ceiling of the display window shows a diluted Ottoman influence.
(PHOTO: THÉRÈSE BONNEY)

WAX MODEL of the American aviator Charles Lindbergh, produced by the Siegel mannequin works. Lindbergh became a French hero when he made a solo flight from the USA to France in 1927. In this window display, he is placed in front of a large aerial photograph of Manhattan skyscrapers, quite the ultimate in modernity.
(PHOTO: THÉRÈSE BONNEY)

3

AVANT-GARDES

*IF YOU ARE LUCKY ENOUGH to have lived in Paris . . . then wherever
you go it stays with you like a movable feast*
ERNEST HEMINGWAY

ATALIE PALEY and Victor Kraft.
Here in a ballet film impro-
visation directed by Pavel Tcheli-
tchev, c.1935. Natalie Paley was
the daughter of Russian exile
Grand Duke Paul. Like so many
of her counterparts, she had
become a fashion model, her then
famished slenderness was envied
by overweight Parisiennes. She
married the couturier Lucien
Lelong and her icy beauty of the
Garbo type was influential in the
Thirties.

(PHOTO: CECIL BEATON)

FTER THE FIRST WORLD WAR, each and every intellectual began to
question the basis of a culture that had managed to produce such
unprecedented barbarity. The poet Paul Valéry solemnly declared: 'We who
incarnate civilisation, know at present that we are mortal'. Nothing was ever
to be stable again: neither the franc, morals, art, fashion nor politics,
everything was subject to instantaneous questioning and imminent
revolution. Already in the middle of the war, in Zurich, the first wave of self-
styled art anarchists created the Dada movement and exploded patriotic
mythology with vitriolic rage: 'Let each man cry out: there is a work of
destruction and negativity to accomplish. Sweep and clean up. The purity
of each individual comes into being after a state of madness, aggressive and
utter madness, in a world left in the hands of bandits who tear at each other
and destroy the work of centuries.'

In his manifesto, Tristan Tzara, one of the main architects of Dada,
expressed better than anyone the romantic yearning to start anew, as if the
war could at least give society a chance to rethink itself. After his arrival in
Paris in December 1919 he became the focal point for French Dada, which
gathered together artists and writers like André Breton, Philippe Soupault,
Louis Aragon and Paul Eluard, all of whom would become the core of the
Surrealist movement. Dada was self-negating and could not ethically
condone any form of structured creativity, but it did serve as a whimsical
measuring-stick for the whole of the avant-garde in the inter-war years.
Though never part of the movement, both Picasso and the composer Erik
Satie always retained an element of the Dada spirit. No solemn statement
about art (or anything else) would be read as definitive ever again.

From the time of Romanticism in the early nineteenth century up to the
interwar years, the distance between the avant-garde and convention had
been steadily growing, as had the love-hate, totally interdependent
relationship between them. Yet, while artists like Picasso, Stravinsky, Léger,
Cocteau and Breton ostensibly offended and outraged, they also thrilled
and inspired. The press thundered, the public writhed in delighted horror,

AYMOND RADIGUET with the pianist Marcelle Meyer in Man Ray's studio on the Rue La Condamine in 1921. Behind them is Man Rays's large painting *Legend* (1916). Raymond Radiguet (1903-23) was a literary prodigy who began publishing poems from the age of 15. Noticed by Max Jacob and taken up by Cocteau, he achieved a considerable career and glory before dying of typhoid at the age of 20. His autobiographical novel *The Devil in the Flesh* (1923) is a masterpiece.

and younger artists gaped and listened. However dismayed they may have been by such outbursts, the bourgeoisie had been nearly as shaken as artists and intellectuals by the implications and consequences of the disastrous world war.

Writers and artists who had experienced the trenches found it hardest to reconcile themselves with the values they had been born with. Patriotism, heroism, belief in a better future, all were defunct. As the critic Jacques Rivière wrote: 'I spend hours going round the table in my hotel room; I walk aimlessly in Paris, I spend entire evenings on a bench in the Place du Châtelet, I live day to day in despondent fatalism'. Others must have felt equally empty. Pierre Drieu la Rochelle, Jean Giono and Louis-Ferdinand Céline, who had all been at the front, reflect this hopelessness in the books they wrote after the war. A frequent hero in interwar literature, from Radiguet to Gide, is the self-doubting amoral adolescent who cannot find meaning in his existence. Céline's *Voyage au Bout de la Nuit* ('Voyage to the End of the Night') of 1932 is perhaps the most powerful book of the Thirties and reverberates with the despairing hollowness of his generation.

Those writers who had any measure of social consciousness worried about the future of society and some members of the avant-garde joined extreme political movements of both the right and left. A literature of convention with matching edifying films attempted to reinstate some kind of French grand tradition, where the class system and catholic tradition triumphed over American-inspired materialism and technology. Escapist travel literature – by Antoine de Saint-Exupéry and Pierre Benoit – was another popular genre, a more adult version of boys' adventure books. Also much favoured were detective stories, a novel import from Britain; the first translations of Agatha Christie began to appear in the late Twenties. The Belgian novelist Georges Simenon, who moved to Paris in 1922, followed suit, and the adventures of Inspector Maigret (at the rate of one a month from 1931 to 1932) turned his creator into the most popular author of his era. The bourgeois reader was becoming incredibly lazy – compared to the pre-war generation – and henceforth demanded facile gratification, rather like the other modes of entertainment competing for his attention.

A related trend was seen in art, leading to a general hostility to the avant-garde in certain quarters, an antipathy that had a political, nationalist edge. People questioned whether the avant-garde had not itself been implicated by the war, suggesting that it had corrupted and undermined French values

PICASSO in his studio 1928. By contrast with his Bohemian pre-war life, in the Twenties Picasso had become a successful, fashionable artist. In 1918 he had married the dancer Olga Koklova from the Ballets Russes. His work of the interwar period was marked by neo-classicism and, of course, Cubism as well as some aspects of Surrealism later. He is shown here in front of his haunting, violent masterpiece *The Dancers* (1925), while on the left is *Painter and Model* (1928).

in the years up to 1914. This became all the more distasteful when it was asserted that much of it had ultimately been the work of 'foreigners' like Picasso. There arose a reactionary urge to restore all that had perished in the trenches, in particular to erase any traces of foreign, especially German, cultural influence. This 'return to order', as it was termed by Cocteau, led to a timid art that tried to locate itself in the line of the great French tradition. Though touched by modern movements, popular painters like Dunoyer de Segonzac produced landscapes and nudes in a late Impressionist mould. Classicism – the essence of everything Latin, Mediterranean and thus French – enjoyed a revival, as seen in the work of André Derain. Picasso himself turned intermittently to a form of neo-classicism in the Twenties, painting large, static nudes that embodied all those values of order and harmony that supposedly defined true French art.

In more enlightened circles and in the wake of Cubism, Futurism, Diaghilev's Ballets Russes and the beginnings of jazz, Paris in the Twenties and Thirties roared and shook from night-club to party and from dance hall to theatre. Society stars such as Poiret, the Count de Beaumont, Winnereta Singer (by now Countess Edmond de Polignac) overreached themselves in prodigious parties where no extravagance was spared. Even more than Diaghilev, Rolf de Maré and his Ballets Suédois were the talk of the town and attracted the collaboration of some of the best artists in Paris.

Artists were involved with every mode of expression including theatre, ballet, opera and cinema, which helps to explain the extraordinary quality of design in the inter-war years. In 1917, for the Ballets Russes, Picasso had worked with the writer and impresario Cocteau and the eccentric composer Erik Satie on what they called a realist ballet, *Parade*, only to be heckled and called *les Trois Boches* ('the three Jerries') by an indignant crowd. By the Twenties, the public expected a certain amount of bewilderment from an avant-garde stage, or movie – but not too much, as was shown by the screening of Dalí and Buñuel's Surrealist film *L'Age d'Or* ('The Golden Age') in 1930. This was interrupted by members of the right-wing Ligue des Patriotes, who threw ink at the screen and destroyed the cinema. Other less controversial collaborations included that for the Ballets Russes production of *Le Train Bleu* ('The Blue Train', 1924) which had a curtain by Picasso, costumes by Chanel, sets by the sculptor Henri Laurens, music by Darius Milhaud (of *Les Six*) and scenario by Cocteau. Matisse produced the décor

*L*E TRAIN BLEU. Produced by Diaghilev's Ballets Russes with music by Darius Milhaud, curtain by Picasso, sets by Laurens and costumes by Chanel. The photograph shows the original cast on the day before the première in June 1924 at the Théatre des Champs-Elysées, and really epitomizes the sporting, flippant Twenties. Cocteau (in the centre) is surrounded, from left to right, by Hilda Munnings (alias Sokolova, the first non-Russian dancer to join Diaghilev's troupe in 1913), Anton Dolin as Beau Gosse in a knitted swim-suit, Leon Woizikovky as the golf-player and Nijinski's foul-tempered sister Bronislava as the tennis player.

BAL DES MATIÈRES, one of the fancy dress balls organised by the Vicomte and Vicomtesse Charles and Marie-Laure de Noailles, the most adventurous art patrons of the age on 19 June 1929. Guests had to arrive in costumes made from paper and refuse. Here Valentine Hugo sports a dress made from paper doyleys and the writer Paul Morand wears a suit of book-covers.

for Stravinsky's one-act ballet, *Le Chant du Rossignol* ('The Song of the Nightingale', 1920).

The avant-garde did not benefit from any state or institutional support and depended on the continuous support of enlightened sponsors. These were found in extremely restricted circles of French upper classes, especially those with artistic and poetic inclinations, like Marie-Laure de Noailles and her husband the Vicomte Charles, who subsidized contemporary music and film. It was they who financed the film *L'Age d'Or*. Comte Etienne de Beaumont was another prominent patron, who financed various of Cocteau's theatrical productions, such as *Le Boeuf sur le Toit* ('The Cow on the Roof', 1920). In these circles the avant-garde and wealthy mixed together in a cosy alliance, the art being just another form of entertainment to add to the round of glittering, offbeat parties they organized. For example, the de Noailles held a number of Bals des Matières, in which all

*A*T MARIE-LAURE DE NOAILLES in 1932. The Vicomte and Vicomtesse de Noailles were among the most eminent and perceptive patrons of the arts in the interwar years. They were the first to commission Robert Mallet-Stevens to build them a villa, in Hyères on the ruins of a medieval monastery. Their elegant Parisian salon, shown here, was decorated by the brilliant Jean-Michel Frank. Marie-Laure is the fourth from the right. Furthest left is the composer Francis Poulenc of *Les Six* and seated next to him, another composer, Charles Koechlin.

the guests had to dress in unusual materials: in 1925 it was synthetic materials like celluloid and vulcanized rubber, in 1929 the guests were dressed entirely in paper and refuse. There were other sources of patronage also: fashion designers such as Chanel and Schiaparelli often collaborated with artists and therefore bought their works. Otherwise, there was American (frequently Sapphic) money: Winnereta Singer, Gertrude Stein especially, and Nathalie Barney were outstanding promoters of the arts in Paris.

What shocked the bourgeoisie often amused the wealthy and aristocratic: the Dadaists and Surrealists courted outrage and publicity. As Breton recalled: 'Enemy Number One was the public at large, we had to get at it through any means and the most direct was scandal. Why not admit that it was scandal that we loved so passionately and that it gave us a reason to live'. They attacked and heckled the sacred cows of the French literary establishment: first the writer Maurice Barrès, then the much-hallowed novelist Anatole France and finally the poet Saint-Pol Roux. In 1921 the group organized a mock trial of the nationalist writer Barrès in which a wooden mannequin was prosecuted by the artists, who were dressed as judges, lawyers and jurors. During the proceedings, Barrès was accused of a 'crime against the safety of the mind'. For France, whose death in 1924 was marked by national mourning, they issued a pamphlet entitled *Un Cadavre*. Aragon's contribution, 'Have you ever Slapped a Dead Man?', ended with the sentence: 'There are days when I dream of an eraser to rub out human filth'. While they felt contempt for France, they actually quite admired Saint-Pol- Roux. Yet the banquet held in his honour in 1925 provoked them to fury after one of the speakers, a notable actress, claimed that 'a Frenchwoman could never marry a German'. Chanting '*A bas la France!*' ('Down with France!'), in the ensuing riot Philippe Soupault swung from the chandeliers, knocking over the wine bottles with his feet, while Breton went around slapping famous writers with his napkin.

Not content to be assaulted by the public alone, the various factions of the avant-garde also squabbled among themselves, jostling for influence within their own circles – politics appeared here as elsewhere. Dada was riven with internal tensions, as was its successor Surrealism: Breton made a habit of 'excommunicating' dissenting voices from the Surrealist movement at regular intervals, filling the gaps with new recruits. Some of the Cubists, who were still thriving in the Twenties, found Dada almost as perplexing and irritating as did the bourgeoisie and attacked it quite as violently as the conservative critics. The painter Albert Gleizes, for example, commented acidly in 1920 that the Dadaists had 'discovered the anus and the by-products of intestinal activity . . . they confuse excrement with the products of the mind'.

Although the police thought otherwise, the Dadaist and Surrealist escapades were part of an attempt to reinvent values for a post-war society. Whatever their nihilistic claims might have been, the Dadaists and even more the Surrealists remained supremely creative artists. Their form of opposition was creation on a hitherto unknown scale: artistic expression were there to save the world from folly in the name of freedom. This social aspect of the art of the interwar period was not limited to these more public manifestations. The Purists, another avant-garde group of the Twenties, centred round the painter Amédée Ozenfant and the painter and architect Le Corbusier, also looked to a future society in their art but were more interested in the machine aesthetic and standardisation. For them the individual destiny would be swallowed up in an ideal mass society – the most ominous of inter-war conceptions. Many abstract artists, like Mondrian or those in the Abstraction-Création group founded in 1931,

*J*OËL MARTEL in front of his villa, 1928. The Martel brothers were friends of Robert Mallet-Stevens. On the ground-floor of their villa was the studio where they produced their sculpture, which was popular at the time, especially inside ocean liners.
(PHOTO: THÉRÈSE BONNEY)

saw their work in the context of grandiose schemes that extended well beyond the narrow limits of a canvas. Mondrian even saw his own obsession with dancing as being of a piece with his austere aesthetic and social theories: for him too the individual would in the future be absorbed into a homogeneous, impersonal whole.

The Surrealists' great innovation was to popularize the more liberating aspects of psychoanalysis: through painting, drawing, films and automatic writing they emphasized instinctual behaviour in opposition to ordered and respectable thinking. This was naturally not the aim of psychoanalysis which was meant to cure the patient from those wilder fantasies that the Surrealists sought to promote as a way of apprehending the world. Aragon, at any rate, thought Freud a hopeless bourgeois. Nevertheless, if only a select élite confessed their dreams on Marie Bonaparte's divan or read Freud works, the general public imbibed a watered-down version of the Oedipus complex or the libido theory in exhibitions and various Surrealist manifestations. The Swiss-born artist Meret Oppenheim's fur-lined teacup and spoon (*Breakfast in Fur*, 1936), Dalí's *Lobster Telephone* (1936, later translated into clothing by Elsa Schiaparelli) became, so to speak, household objects of popular imagination which crossed boundaries and frontiers. The public had integrated this into an all-over cultural experience.

*A*NTONIN ARTAUD in *Les Cenci* at the Folies Wagram theatre, May 1935. An extreme, tortured personality, Artaud (1896-1948) was a writer, actor and dramatist on the fringes of the Surrealist movement (which he left in 1926 when Breton aligned the Surrealists with Communism). His concept of a 'Theatre of Cruelty', as first described in 1932, was focused on the creation of a violent, mystical experience in which the audience would commune with the emotions expressed on stage. *Les Cenci*, written by Artaud but based on Shelley's play of the same name, was far ahead of its time and largely misunderstood.

HP 85
MERCER NEW YORK
1920

FRANCIS PICABIA and Tristan Tzara in Paris, 1920. Romanian-born Tzara (1896-1963) had moved to Paris at the end of the preceeding year from Zurich where he had co-founded the Dada movement in 1916. His close friend, the anarchic Picabia (1879-1953), came from a wealthy background and had a passion for cars: this one is an American Mercer. He founded and ran the Dada periodical *391* (1917- 24). The two Dada artists joined the poets Breton, Soupault, Eluard and Aragon in the circle around the magazine *Littérature* (1919-23). A year later, when Picabia officially left the group (taking his financial support with him), Cocteau remarked: 'After a long con-valescence, Picabia is now recovered. I really saw Dada creep out of his eye'.

From 1930 onwards, Mickey Mouse, Dick Tracy and Johnny Weissmuller provided as much as excitement as any Surrealist extravaganza, probably more so as movies had made these outlandish little heroes far more accessible.

During the inter-war years art provided a popular sort of entertainment, woven into the fabric of everyday life. Even the Dadaists did not entirely manage to irritate the bourgeois public – in fact some quite liked their absurd, spectacular events. Their 'Premier Vendredi de Littérature' (*Littérature* was the name of the French Dadaist journal), which took place on 23 January 1920, drew a large audience. The performers included Tzara's *Poème* in which he read straight from a newspaper article to the accompaniment of a cacophony of bells and rattles. Tickets were sold for such events – some quite expensive – and as well as their own publicity, they were advertised in the national press. The audience enjoyed themselves throwing rubbish at the stage – on one occasion escalopes and beef steaks bought from a local butcher in the interval. It proved very hard to retain the power to outrage. Ironically, during the internal squabbles at the end of Dada's life in France, the artists annoyed each other more than anyone else. At the 'Soirée du Coeur à Barbe' in July 1923, organized by Tzara alone, Breton appeared with Benjamin Péret and Aragon and started attacking the

performers. During the ensuing struggle, one of the participants broke an arm before Breton and his cronies were dragged off.

Such publicly successful spectacles were continued by the Surrealists, notably at the International Exhibition of Surrealism, which was held at the Galerie des Beaux-Arts for two months in 1938 and organized by Duchamp (who disappeared to England only hours before the opening). Among other delights, it advertised the presence of 'echoes' and 'perfumes from Brazil' (produced by a coffee roaster). Inside, loudspeakers played German marching songs and braziers lit the central exhibition space. There was a 'Surrealist Street' consisting of a line of female dummies dressed by various artists – Duchamp, Man Ray, Max Ernst, Dalí, Miró and others. At the entrance to the show, Dalí placed an old dilapidated taxi, which had a mannequin driver with a shark's head. In the back seat was a blonde doll seated on a bed of lettuce with hundreds of snails crawling everywhere. A sprinkler ensured that the exhibit (called 'Rainy Taxi') and its spectators were kept drenched throughout.

One of the most accessible art forms was fashion, especially as artists and designers worked together. Previously, clothing had been an expression of social conformity or, at its most imaginative, a way of advertising financial success and ambition. Not, of course, that this stopped – one merely

HÉLÈNE VANEL dancing 'the bicycle-archbishop dance' at the opening of the Surrealist exhibition, 1938. During the vernissage, it was rumoured that one Enigmarelle, son of Frankenstein, would come to the show at half-past midnight. Whilst waiting, the dancer Hélène Vanel offered a performance around and in the lily pond at the centre of the gallery. Third from the left is Man Ray, while beside Vanel, with his back turned, is Dalí. On the floor is a mass of leaves and moss, another of Duchamp's ideas.

E P'TIT PARIGOT, costumes and scenery by Sonia Delaunay, Albert Gleizes and André Lhote, film by René le Somptier, 1926. A three-dimensional Cubist extravaganza. Film was one of the most exciting ways to experiment with contemporary art, and in the inter-war period there were marvellous collaborations between artists and adventurous film-makers. Despite the attempts of their politically conscious producers, these films never made it to the box-office and were restricted to artistic circles and the patrons who sponsored them

flaunted wealth in a more minimalist disguise. Post-cubist fabrics, folksy embroidery (by Lanvin) hand-knits (by Schiaparelli), Chanel's deadpan cashmeres all cost a fortune but also made sure that the wearer was (nearly) as culturally innovative as the designer. This was especially so if she had made the effort to be suitably slim and bronzed (with the help of Helena Rubinstein's Creme Gipsy foundation), with hair bobbed and eye brows pencilled, a cross between a Modigliani, Natalie Paley and Yvonne Printemps at her most flippant. Fashion houses paid glamorous albeit impoverished East European princesses, known as *mannequins de ville*, to flaunt their creations at premières, *vernissages* or on the race-tracks. And Haute Couture fashion shows were marvellous spectacles for which heiresses and would-be gigolos crossed the Atlantic. In the Thirties, the shows were scheduled in accordance with the arrivals of liners from the United States and South America.

Some artistic enterprises proved quite commercial. Sonia Delaunay, working with the couturier Jacques Heim, provided patchwork designs, which she called simultanist (after the theory of Simultanism adopted by her husband Robert and others before the war). Sold at their boutique, which ran from 1925 to 1929, these were the equivalent of the jazz age for fabrics and were even transposed onto a car, the Citroën 5CV. During the

1925 Arts Décoratifs exhibition, they ran a *boutique simultanée* on the Alexander IIIrd bridge, and hordes of visitors snapped up the patchwork pullovers and coats on display. In the same year, the Futurist artist Fortunato Depero launched a line of lavishly embroidered waistcoats which he presented in a fashion show starring fellow-futurist Marinetti on the top of the Eiffel Tower. Restaurants were eagerly decorated by famous artists: the still-legendary Coupole, synonymous with Bohemian Montparnasse and opened in 1927, flaunts pillars by Léger, Kisling and Marie Wassilieff.

In the growing consumer society, eager to pay for its new-found leisure, literature, too, became merely a cultural product and publishing houses invented prizes and promoted their books with advertisements (just the same as for laxatives, one haughty critic observed). Such lavish launching served the popularity of the rapidly infamous novel *La Garçonne* (1922) by Victor Margueritte and even more Raymond Radiguet's *Le Diable au Corps* ('The Devil in the Flesh') which came out a year later. The famed Nancy Cunard, heiress to her father's floating empire ran the Hours Press, one of the rare successful presses of the period. On a seventeenth-century hand press, she printed marvellous editions of Ezra Pound and Samuel Beckett. She too was an avid collector of contemporary and particularly Surrealist works.

Art and literature were henceforth in competition with every other form of entertainment. The public could choose between Francis Poulenc and Louis Armstrong, Germaine Tailleferre and Damia, André Gide and Gaston Leroux, theatre and the movies. If a middling bourgeoisie went eagerly to everything on show, others restricted themselves to options dictated by class and social expectation. The *jeunesse dorée*, old rich or *nouveau*, voraciously sought multifarious entertainment, and more and more of it as the decade wore thin. On the same day, you might have gone to a boxing match, hummed *Boum quand mon coeur fait boum* ('Bang, my heart goes Bang', Charles Trenet's lead hit) on your way to a Surrealist exhibition at their gallery on the Rue Callot before spending a wild night at the Bal Nègre, a black cabaret with jazz in the then-dingy Rue Blomet, a stone's throw from the abattoirs.

*R*OBERT DELAUNAY in his studio at 19 Boulevard Malesherbes in an elegant quarter of the Right Bank, 1924/5. In the background is a wall hanging embroidered with a poem by the Surrealist Philippe Soupault, made by Sonia in 1922. On the inside of both halves of the door is a poem by Vladimir Mayakovsky (1893-1930), who was in Paris at this time (October 1924-January 1925). The Delaunays' home, work and life-style threw a perfect bridge between contemporary art in Paris and Moscow.
(PHOTO: THÉRÈSE BONNEY)

*S*CENE from the Ballets Russes production of *Le Train Bleu* in 1924 (*above*). The ballet was about the smart-set on holiday in the South of France and shows the influence of sport, which was one of the real novelties of the Twenties, affecting both life-styles and fashion. Henri Laurens created Cubist bathing cabins for the sets, while Chanel designed the costumes - bright modern jerseys, adventurous bathing suits, sandals and golfing shoes - all of which created a sensation.

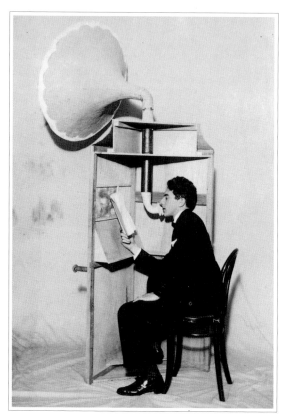

*J*EAN COCTEAU during a rehearsal for the mime play *Les Mariés de la Tour Eiffel*, 1921 (*right*). He is seen here reading the text through one of the two 'Phonographes'. In touch with every avant-garde movement, which he plundered for inspiration, Cocteau (1889-1963) was the supreme art impresario and culture catalyst of the interwar period. He wrote poems and librettos, designed sets, drew and made legendary films, providing a bridge between these different arts and inventing a uniquely fluent style. The Surrealists thought he confused freedom with fickleness and despised him for it.

*T*HE BALLETS SUÉDOIS at the foot of the Eiffel Tower on the 22 June 1922 with its star dancer Jean Börlin and friends and collaborators, including Cocteau, Leon Bakst, Irène Lagut, Jean and Valentine Hugo, Désiré Ingelbrecht, Paul Morand and four members of *Les Six*: Francis Poulenc, Arthur Honegger, Georges Auric and Germaine Tailleferre. The Ballets Suédois founded by Rolf de Maré were even more popular in the Twenties than the legendary Ballets Russes. The writer Ricciotto Canudo tried to explain the difference: 'Their charm is slow. The blonde heads of the dancers shine with lunar pallor, they move gently with none of the dark savage frenzy of the Slavs'.

*T*HE LAVISH wedding feast scene from the Ballets Suédois production of *Les Mariés de la Tour Eiffel* at the Théâtre des Champs Elysées on 18 June 1921 (*above*). The libretto was by Jean Cocteau, the scenery by Irène Lagut, and the costumes and masks by Jean Hugo. The music was composed by five of *Les Six* (all but Durey of: Darius Milhaud, Georges Auric, Louis Durey, Arthur Honegger, Francis Poulenc and Germaine Tailleferre), who Cocteau promoted and who were influenced by the neo-classicism of Satie and Stravinsky. The première of the ballet was disrupted by Tzara and other Dadaists. (PHOTO: ISABEY)

*L*E BOEUF SUR LE TOIT, a farce written by Jean Cocteau, with music by Milhaud, sets and costumes by Dufy (who took over after the death of Guy Fauconnet), February 1920 (*right*). Sponsored by the Count de Beaumont, it was performed at the Comédie des Champs Elysées and the actors included the three Fratellini clowns. *Le Boeuf sur le Toit* was later the name Cocteau gave to a legendary bar which opened in 1922 near the Place de la Concorde, the haunt where Radiguet, Gide and Mistinguett frequently drank.

CARYATHIS (alias Elise Jouhandeau) dancing to Satie's *La Belle Excentrique* at the Théatre du Colisée on 15 June 1921. She wears a costume designed by Cocteau and made by Poiret. The music was far more adventurous than the costume and despite its ironic, misleading simplicity, it influenced not only *Les Six* but even Stravinsky.

SKATING RINK performed by the Ballets Suédois, a *poème dansé*, with libretto by Canudo, music by Honegger, and sets and costumes by Fernand Léger as performed on 20 January 1922 at the Théâtre des Champs Elysées. Contemporary art was a form of total entertainment of the most exciting, if elitist, kind.

SCENE from André Gide's play *Saül* staged by Jacques Copeau at the Théâtre du Vieux Colombier, 16 June 1922, with music by Arthur Honegger (*above*). Since the end of the war, this theatre was famous for concerts of avant-garde music given by Honegger and his friends in *Les Six*. It was certainly unusual for such a restrained intellectual and anxious Protestant as Gide (1869-1951) to partake in such an extravagant production. *Saül* as a play is exceptional in his long career and, though published in 1903, this was its first production in France.

PAUL POIRET (right) and André Derain (1880-1954) (*opposite*). Having been one of the leading Fauve painters (with Matisse and others) before the war, Derain turned to a more traditional, 'neo-classical' style in the Twenties in a manner typical of the 'return to order' of that period. One wishes that his friend, the couturier Poiret, had done the same instead of feigning youthful novelty to the end.

HENRI LAURENS in his studio with the sculpture *Standing Woman with Drapery*, c.1927-8 (*above*). The sculptor and engraver Laurens (1885-1954) worked in the Cubist tradition and was a life-long friend of Braque. His nymphs and goddesses are perhaps the most modern statement of the classic female form the sculpture of the period produced. (PHOTO: THÉRÈSE BONNEY)

DERAIN with a model in 1935 (*opposite*). Derain's balanced and harmonious postwar paintings epitomize what was termed the French School in opposition to the 'foreign' School of Paris. The female nude constituted a crucial element of this classical aesthetic. Like many other artists of the period, he also created stage décor for ballets, including those performed by the Ballets Russes. (PHOTO: ANDRÉ ROGI)

MARCEL DUCHAMP (1887-1968) in 1938. Here shown with a with chess-board on his wall, Duchamp was probably the most independent artist of the twentieth century with the most influential and challenging conception of art. Throughout his life he kept up a true Dada spirit in all his activities, including chess, which remained his passion. In 1938 he masterminded the Surrealist Exhibition. (PHOTO: DENISE BELLON)

*F*ERNAND LÉGER in his studio at 86 Rue Notre Dame des Champs, 1930. Léger (1881-1955) began as an innovative Cubist painter and after the war showed an increasing interest in machines, which he perceived as the liberators of mankind. He was committed to socialism all his life. Behind him are two of the three panels (*Comet Tails on a Black Ground*) that he was painting as a screen for the American artist Gerald Murphy (1888-1964) to go in his villa in Antibes. Murphy had arrived in Paris in 1921 and, like Léger, had collaborated with the Ballets Suédois.
(PHOTO: THÉRÈSE BONNEY)

Sonia delaunay and models in Robert Delaunay's studio, c.1925 (*above*). Paintings by Robert (1885-1941) and clothes by his wife Sonia (née Terk, 1885-1979) which she wears (right). By the time the 1925 Arts Décoratifs exhibition took place, the couple had created a completely coherent style together. Before the First World War Robert had been dubbed an Orphist painter by the poet Guillaume Apollinaire and he continued in this mode (an offshoot of Cubism) thereafter. The large painting in the background with its concentric colour discs is typical of his mature style. The inclusion of an aeroplane (still a novelty) and the Eiffel Tower are also characteristic.

Sonia delaunay (right) and a model in Robert Delaunay's studio, c.1925 (*opposite*). Sonia's interest in fabrics dates back from the days when their son Charles was a baby in 1911, when she made a patchwork quilt for him. She designed costumes for the Ballets Russes and came to create highly popular fabrics inspired by her husband's work.

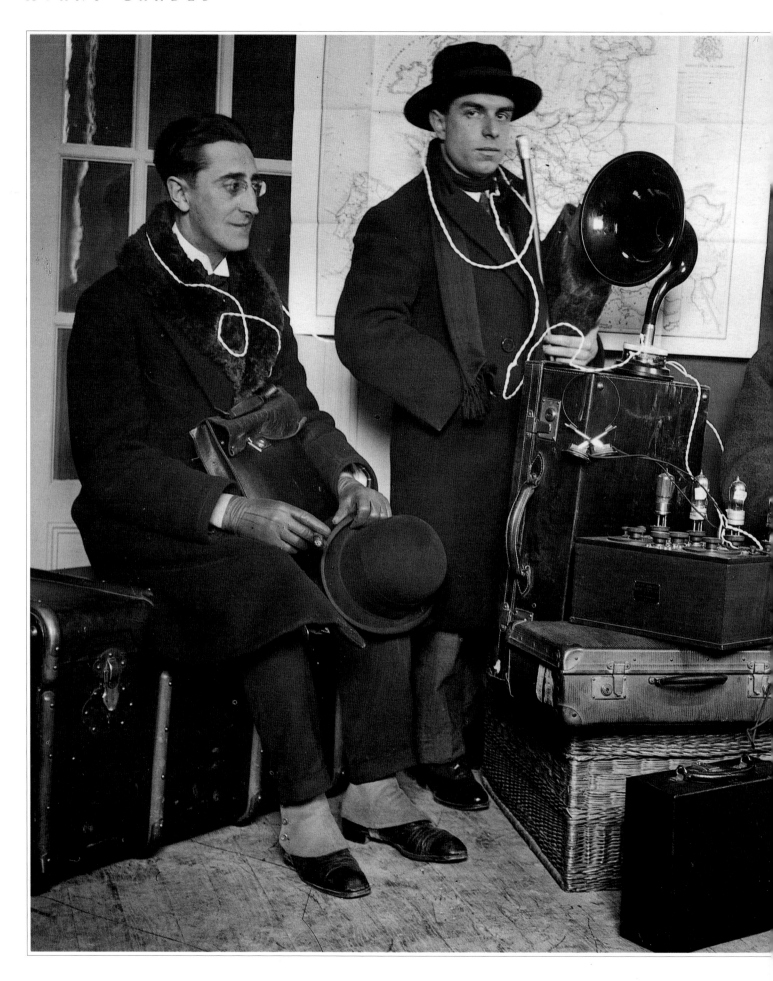

*T*HE AMERICAN BORN sculptor Alexander Calder (1898-1976) in his studio, at 7 Rue de Cels, 1928-30 (*above*). Calder moved from New York to Paris in 1926 and alternated between France and the USA throughout the interwar period. A member of the eclectic association of abstract artists, Abstraction-Création, from its foundation in 1931, he experimented with moving metal sculptures, which were activated by electricity or by hand. Duchamp named these 'mobiles', while the sculptor Hans Arp called the non-moving sculptures 'stabiles'.
(PHOTO: THÉRÈSE BONNEY)

*P*AUL DERMÉE (left), Enrico Prampolini (centre) and Michel Seuphor (right) with their radiophone, c.1927 (*left*). Dermée, once a Dadaist, was a co-founder of the Purist journal *L'Esprit Nouveau*, Prampolini (1894-1956) was an Italian Futurist artist, architect and experimenter who regularly visited Paris from 1925 to 1937, and the writer Seuphor (an anagram of 'Orpheus') was a devoted supporter of abstract art. In France and elsewhere at this time there was much interest in creating bizarre electronic music devices (especially among the Futurists), most of which proved worthless as instruments.
(PHOTO: ANDRÉ KERTESZ)

*D*ADA ARTISTS, contributors to the magazines *Littérature* and *391*, c.1920 (*above*). From left to right, in the first row: Tzara, Céline Arnauld, Picabia and Breton; second row: Dermée, Soupault, Ribemont-Dessaignes; third row: Aragon, Théodore Fraenkel, Eluard, Clément Pansaers, Faÿ.

*E*XPOSITION DADA MAX ERNST, 1921 (*right*). This was taken during the *vernissage* of the Max Ernst exhibition at the Au Sans Pareil gallery in the Avenue Kléber on 2 May 1921, with from left to right: Breton, Soupault, Jacques Rigaut, Benjamin Péret and Serge Charchoune. The show mainly included Dada collages, with strange titles such as *The Hat Makes the Man*, and greatly impressed the French Dadaists. It was not until the following year that Ernst came to Paris from Cologne.

A DADA EVENING c.1921. Wearing his usual monocle is Tzara, with the word 'DADA' inscribed on his forehead. Among the others shown are Auric (furthest right), and Georges Ribemont-Dessaignes (furthest left, standing), with 'Dada' written on his face, and standing next to him, Picabia. This group would meet every Sunday in the Rue Emile Augier along with Eluard, Jean Crotti and Aragon to plan the week's scandals. As their friend André Breton wrote: 'Why not admit that it was scandal we loved so passionately and that it gave us a reason to live.'

*T*HE SURREALIST EXHIBITION. This extravagant venture opened at the Galerie des Beaux-Arts on the elegant Rue du Faubourg Saint-Honoré on 17 January 1938 and was coordinated by Marcel Duchamp. On the ceiling are the much-publicized '1,200 coal sacks' following Duchamp's idea. Flanked by an Yves Tanguy painting, the door on the left leads into the 'Surrealist Street' of mannequins. (PHOTO: DENISE BELLON)

*V*IEW of the 'Surrealist Street' at the Surrealist exhibition, 1938. At the centre is Dalí's bird-headed mannequin, in front of a mass of publicity about the artist (he was a supreme self-publicist). The next one down is a mannequin with a bat on its head, by Wolfgang Paalen (1907-59).

D ALÍ putting the finishing touches on his mannequin for the 'Surrealist Street' at the 1938 Surrealist exhibition. The Surrealist interest in female mannequins (seen most disconcertingly in the mangled, dislocated works of Bellmer) was merely one aspect of their general fascination with sexuality. (PHOTO: DENISE BELLON)

A 'WAKING DREAM' session among the Surrealists, 1924. From left to right are: Max Morise, Roger Vitrac, Jacques-André Boiffard, André Breton, Paul Eluard, Pierre Naville, Giorgio de Chirico and Philippe Soupault. In front: Simone Collinet, Robert Desnos and Jacques Baron. The touchstone of Surrealism was the unconscious and one means of gaining access to it was through self-induced trance states in which one could directly recite a 'waking dream'. Desnos was one of the most susceptible to these states and here provides the focus to the meeting. As to whether such states were genuine, Aragon said 'Is simulating a thing any different from thinking it? And what one thinks exists.' The photo is by the American Man Ray (1890-1976), himself prominent in these circles.

4

LIVING THE LIFE
IN PARIS

In Paris there's a lady
She has teeth of gold, many servants
Plentiful admirers. A garden on her roof
Fish in her bath. Fantastical jewellery
Birds from Brazil. An Alaskan fox stole
CHARLES TRENET: *'DANS PARIS Y A UNE DAME'* (1935)

I N THE INTERWAR PERIOD, France was turning from a predominantly rural country into an urban society, with a large middle class full of new expectations. Henceforth, the bourgeoisie would be the role-model for design and people's lifestyles. The poor aspired towards domesticated middle-class luxury, which they imitated with bakelite and rayon instead of ivory and silk. Likewise the wealthy sought discretion through bourgeois guise and it was no longer advisable to flaunt one's tiara in the midst of 'Bolshie' agitation. As Chanel purportedly said in a much paraphrased sentence: never mind if your diamonds are real as long as they look fake. Style became synonymous with elegance, and the nouveau pauvre, the new streamlined chic, was the fashion. An alarmed Maurice Barrès cried 'there are no social classes left'. For the older generation, a crowd uniformly clad in short dresses, cloche hats and gaberdine coats running from metro to office to cinema must have indeed seemed classless, sporting a look called 'ready to wear' that was supplied by the main stores.

MME MATHIEU-LÉVY, c.1928-9. Madame Mathieu-Lévy, known as Suzanne Talbot, bought the famous milliner's store to which she gave her name in 1917. Here she is clad in a *robe de style* reminiscent of the *Gazette du Bon-Ton*, a cascade of pastel chiffon petals on spectacular high heels. Her apartment on the Rue Lota in the 16th *arrondissement* was decorated by Eileen Gray (from 1919) and was all silver and grey with tinted mirrors and lacquered furniture.

(PHOTO: THÉRÈSE BONNEY)

The city was more than a utilitarian alternative to the country, it was the only place to be in, the centre of money, culture and entertainment. Gone forever were the sinuous extravagances of Art Nouveau (henceforth known as the *style nouille* – noodle style) so typical of the Belle-Epoque, which were perceived as being as decadent and as *passé* as the élite they serviced. Yet despite the phenomenal urban expansion, there was little or no town planning. Cumbersome legislation hardly encouraged any new building in the Twenties. Until the beginning of World War One, housing for the working-classes had been a private and haphazard matter. The number of houses built lagged chronically behind the ever-growing number of immigrants. In a massive and continuous revamp of the city, more and more buildings were pulled down to make room for avenues and vistas. Socialist and Radical members of parliament pushed for new decrees enabling the

City of Paris itself to build public housing. The thirty-five kilometres of fortifications put up in the 1840s round Paris were pulled down for this purpose. During the inter-war period, some 53,000 apartments were erected of varying quality in and around Paris, though this was only about half the amount needed. These were the famed *Habitations à Bon Marché* (HBM, literally cheap housing) and much thinking went into rationalizing the narrow spaces allocated to the architects.

Most Parisians were housed in old buildings with, at best, cold water on each floor. Despite the stereotype of life in marvellous Art Deco surroundings, most people lived in near-Victorian conditions. Nevertheless, they began to skimp and save to buy furniture and household appliances as never before. Young people actually had money to spend on the new, relatively cheap consumer products on display in the shops and department stores. The furniture at shops such as Levitan or Le Studio du Meuble was a kind of modernistic, pasteurized Art Deco. Equally alluring were all the electrical kitchen appliances, especially the light-weight electric iron, a far cry from the burning, heavy cast iron variety. Washing machines and refrigerators provided domestic dream material as gas and electricity continued to be prohibitively expensive in France: in the Thirties consumption per inhabitant in France was about one fifth of what it was in Britain and one twelfth of what was usual in the USA. Pattern books for dress making and knitting were extremely popular in the lower-middle classes, and every magazine had a crafts supplement. Designer clothes were described in a such a way as to be intelligible to eager dress-makers. Fashion demanded fastidious attention and continuous care: even working-class children were sent off to school with properly ironed smocks from which perkily embroidered collars emerged.

Liberation was for the wealthy, preferably those idle enough to enjoy cocktail parties, endless telephone conversations and *une américaine* perched in one of those rings that doubled up as a cigarette holder. Indeed telephones were a luxury, and people went to the local café to make calls. In 1932, in a show of artistic extravagance, Marcel Duchamp, in his Russian chess club by the Place Pigalle, played two rounds of a tournament by telephone with Buenos-Aires.

In the new society of the post-war period, architects and designers had to rethink the conventional ideas about housing and town-planning.

*L*E CORBUSIER (1887-1965) in his studio, c.1937. Born in Switzerland, his real name was Charles-Edouard Jeanneret and he lived in Paris from 1917. With Amedée Ozenfant he was one of the founders of Purism, and examples of his Purist paintings can be seen in the background. He was also a pioneer of modernist architecture, as he showed with his innovative, but much decried, Pavillon de l'Esprit Nouveau at the 1925 International Exhibition. (PHOTO: ANDRÉ ROGI)

Architects like Le Corbusier, suitably alarmed by what was going on, realized that one could not go on expanding the city in the Twentieth century without careful thought. Social unrest and the Russian revolution forced architects to broaden their attitudes and relate whatever they built to an over-all (preferably ideal) environment, all the more so as the present one was so disquieting. It was henceforth impossible to create in a void, for a select élite only, since each human existence was thought to be somehow bound up with the destiny of society as a whole.

Paradoxically, despite the appalling uses to which it had been put during the war, machinery and technology were seized upon by many artists as a solution to the period's problems and had a potent influence on design and architecture. Like the Futurists before the war, the machine, in particular the motor-car, fuelled fantasy in every realm of creation from art to the movies. Le Corbusier thought the house 'a machine for living in', Duchamp devised his mechanistic work the 'Large Glass' (1915-23), Marcel L'Herbier produced the film *L'Inhumaine* ('The Heartless Woman', 1923) in collaboration with Robert Mallet-Stevens and Fernand Léger, Léger himself created the film *Ballet Mécanique* ('Mechanical Ballet', 1924) and Jean Cocteau wrote the play *La Voix Humaine* ('The Human Voice', 1930), where the hero is a telephone in the middle of the stage. Opposition to this

*F*AÇADE of the offices of *La Semaine à Paris* in the Rue d'Assas, c.1930. Designed by Robert Mallet-Stevens (1928-9), the series of glass and metal rectangles (by Louis Barillet) is organized into seven panels. Each one bears the name of one of the days of the week and a depiction of a particular leisure activity - an evening at the theatre, a concert, dining out and so on - reflecting the focus of this weekly newspaper.
(PHOTO: THÉRÈSE BONNEY)

ALFA-ROMEO showroom in the Rue Marbeuf. Designed (1925) by Mallet-Stevens, the façade is influenced by Le Corbusier and Rietveld. The design of the porches is redolent of the then fashionable bakelite radios. Mallet-Stevens delighted in the chance to design a building especially for cars, which were a great influence on his design. (PHOTO: THÉRÈSE BONNEY)

aesthetic, as in films like Abel Gance's *La Roue* ('The Wheel', 1923), was rare within the avant-garde.

In *L'Inhumaine* one of the protagonists is an engineer, Einar Noorsen, whose twin passions are sport and modern science. The architectural sets by Mallet-Stevens were intended to provide a suitably modern, machine-look to the film as did Léger's design for the laboratory in the interior scenes. Mallet-Stevens's approach towards architecture was typical of the avant-garde modernism of the period, as expressed in his comment of 1922: 'Apartment blocks, public buildings, workers' housing, the wealthiest villas will in the future be designed in the same spirit as factories'. The fetishistic adoration for the car occasionally found its perfect outlet for expression: in 1925, for example, Mallet-Stevens designed the Alfa Romeo showroom in the Rue Marbeuf. Le Corbusier's pioneering book *Vers une architecture* ('Towards an Architecture', 1923) includes an image of a car in front of the Parthenon, as though the former had somehow superseded the latter. Le Corbusier and the artists in his circle like Léger and Ozenfant perceived the machine as the supreme liberator of mankind from chaos. The house was indeed a machine to live in, all slabs of concrete, rectilinear lines, white on gray, inspired by Greek architecture and the minimalist lines of Japanese thought and artifacts. His most durable contribution is doubtless the notion of the habitat as comprised of basic units that could be multiplied according to need and circumstance. The belief was that despite every technological change, human needs remained the same and could be wholly rationalized.

The classic modernist forms Le Corbusier gave his buildings remain quite distinct from the more anecdotal decorative features on contemporary housing. Yet modernist aesthetics proved far too stark for most people who preferred the garishness of Art Deco, the tango oranges, the endless greens, the aubergines and all the decorative detailing that invaded every surface: packaging of any kind, be it cement, paper or even face-powder was as elaborate as what it concealed. The design of household objects, perfume bottles, cars, ships, aeroplanes as well as typography and shop-fronts were subject to similar criteria. Whereas the modernist style was the result of a radical rethinking of the social environment, Art Deco was by contrast all surface and veneer. Its sources were eclectic and indiscriminate – it was a 'look' rather than an aesthetic. Though Art Deco was celebrated at the 1925 International Exhibition, it was by then somewhat *passé*, its seeds having been sown before the war. Yet, the French tradition of luxury design and an unwillingness to take note of anything emanating from outside, especially from the German Bauhaus, meant that modernism was slow to take root. However, by the late Twenties it was on the ascendant and a greater austerity became *de rigueur*.

Architects, especially Pierre Patout and Mallet-Stevens, borrowed their forms from cars, planes and especially steamers. In fact, with furniture designer Jacques-Emile Ruhlmann, Patout decorated luxurious steamers, the *Ile-de-France*, the *Atlantique* in the late Twenties and the legendary *Normandie* in the mid-Thirties. This exorcised the sinister reminiscence of the *Titanic* and henceforth the most fashionable *mondains* pretended to live on deck, even in the midst of Parisian roof-tops. Even in town houses, port-hole windows were all the rage, and terraces were adorned with tubular furniture, airline lamps and huge paintings by Purist artists representing spare parts of some mythological machinery. The sleek lines of machines were flaunted in posters also, notably those of Cassandre: his famous advertisement for the *Normandie* seems almost an emblem of the period.

Chanel, Madeleine Vionnet and Alix Grès provided the matching apparel topped with metal jewellery, preferably glossed ball bearings or bakelite

CITROËN Automobile showroom, 32 Rue Marbeuf, before 1929 when it was demolished. Designed by Albert Laprade and E. L. Bazin, the large glass curtain wall permitted an over-all view of the cars, which were displayed on balconies. The architects conceived this showroom as a theatre stage.
(PHOTO: THÉRÈSE BONNEY)

*T*HE SALON DE COIFFURE Lina Cavalieri, inside view. The lady is having her nails done at a pastiche Louis XV desk but the possibly genuine armchair gives the salon an air of discernment. The lights are a curious survival from the Art Nouveau period. The display on glass shelves, complete with concealed lighting is the ultimate in chic: the scent bottles and cosmetic jars are made to look like priceless art works.
(PHOTO: THÉRÈSE BONNEY)

bullets. Technology was brought into the realm of beauty, a new-found science: there were machines to slim and tone, curl one's hair, iron out the wrinkles, as if sheer electricity guaranteed immortality. A visit to one of these institutions was a definite sign of modernity. After the war, hairdressers, seamstresses, manicurists, even perfumers, continued to come to wealthy homes, but the demand was such that they gradually began to set up shops all over Paris, catering for the middle- and working-classes. Beauty became an industry, slimming an obligation, permanent youth an absolute law, even if it meant agonising skin-peeling sessions and skull-scorching perms. With the help of *Marie-Claire*, *Modes et Travaux* and *Confidences*, clothing, make-up, life-style all were amalgamated into a scheme of fashion and social acceptability. Beauty parlours were such an attractive investment that even the writer Colette briefly opened one that specialized in aroma-therapy.

Those who could afford it had interiors designed for them that reflected their ideals and aspirations. Artists and art collectors would probably commission minimalist housing from the likes of Le Corbusier or Mallet-Stevens as they needed novel spatial arrangements to house modernist art works. In other cases, the result could be less predictable. Else Schiaparelli, the most baroque of all couturiers, had her apartment arranged Spartan-style by Jean-Michel Frank, as did Madeleine Vionnet: white walls, curtains and chairs, set off by an orange leather settee, green divans and black square tables, a stark concept when compared to her clothes. And yet when Chanel came to visit, 'she shuddered as if she were passing a cemetery', Schiaparelli recalled, even though one might have expected the opposite, given the terse geometric lines of her clothes. Coco preferred the lavishness of antique furniture and art-works in her home.

Boutiques were the ideal place to flaunt one's taste and advertise the titillating aspects of the modernity on sale. The most dazzling example was the hairdresser Antoine's salon (completed 1927), a glass house on four floors, where the exterior walls were replaced with sheets of opaque glass. Even the staircase was glass, and the building serviced Antoine's carefully publicized extravaganzas. To celebrate its opening, Antoine held a 'White Ball' to which 1400 guests came, each of them sent an invitation engraved on glass and wrapped in parchment. Mallet- Stevens was commissioned to design the façades of a number of shops and bars, for example the Bally

shoe store in the Boulevard de la Madeleine (1928) and the Café du Brésil in the Boulevard Haussmann (1930). Many bars, clubs and store fronts with lesser budgets made a feature of the lettering in the window or on the door and incorporated it in the over-all design of the premises. Even department stores built in the early years of the century revamped their window displays in Art Deco fashion.

On the whole, avant-garde building and design was occasional and scattered. One notable exception, however, was the Rue Mallet-Stevens, designed and built by Mallet-Stevens from 1925 to 1927, which allowed for a more complete exposition of modernism. Located in Auteil, an elegant quarter of Paris in the 16th *arrondissement*, this cul-de-sac contains an entire group of houses and villas, both for the architect himself and his clients, whom he had persuaded to buy adjoining plots for this very purpose. The interiors were designed by Mallet-Stevens, Pierre Chareau, Francis Jourdain and others and the whole project was opened with much pomp and ceremony in 1927 by a Minister and two Prefects.

Just as Art Deco eventually gave way to modernism, so in the Thirties, for those who could afford it in the Depression, Surrealism became an influence on design. The art patron Carlos de Beistegui's penthouse apartment in Paris was built by Le Corbusier in the early Thirties but he

ROBERT MALLET-STEVENS'S own villa, 12 Rue Mallet-Stevens, 1928. Designed for himself in 1927, this shows the epitomy of his style with its ocean liner curved walls. Each of the houses he designed on this street remained individual while relating to the overall ensemble.
(PHOTO: THÉRÈSE BONNEY)

*L*ES PARFUMS ISABEY, before 1928, designed by Charles Siclis. Many of the glass perfume containers of the period were works of art in their own right and were specially commissioned from the likes of René Lalique, names normally associated with La Belle Epoque. The façade shows the increasing fascination with sheet glass barely suspended by metallic framing, a technical miracle of the time.

(PHOTO: THÉRÈSE BONNEY)

found its stark aesthetic too outmoded by then and instead had it redone in a more ornamental and bizarre Surrealist style. Grass was laid on the flat roof, around the sides of which he placed imitation baroque furniture, creating the effect of a room with an unusual carpet and no ceiling. The rest of the building was kitted out with peculiar electrical gadgets that made whole walls disappear at the touch of a button.

Aside from their collaborative work on interiors, artists also contributed to modern architecture by commissioning experimental buildings from the avant-garde architects of their day. Auguste Perret designed magnificent work spaces with vast expanses of glass and concrete facing for artists as different as Cassandre (1924), Chana Orloff (1926) and Braque (1927), Orloff's being Perret's first frame house in reinforced concrete. What emerged was a remarkable unity of urban style uniquely Parisian in quality which has come to characterise not just *l'entre-deux-guerres* but the Ville-Lumière itself.

*L*ÉGER in the scenery workshops of the film *L'Inhumaine* (1923) in 1924 (*above*). Unlike Fritz Lang in *Metropolis* (1926), Fernand Léger did not attempt to build a science-fiction set, but tried to suggest the world of the future through parts of machinery used for decorative ends: perforated metal plates, girders and grids, a monumental three-dimensional version of his own paintings

*T*HE SCULPTORS Joël and Jan Martel in their studio, c.1926 (*opposite*). The large drawing on the wall shows the Monument to Claude Debussy (who had died in 1918) which was designed in collaboration with the architect Jean Burkhalter and was built in the forest of Saint-Germain-en-Laye in 1932. It is inspired by Egyptian architecture, like so many of the other sculptures made after Tutenkhamen's tomb was uncovered in 1922. The table is covered with typical decorative Art Deco sculpture. For all their modernity, the brothers are still wearing traditional artists' smocks. (PHOTO: THÉRÈSE BONNEY)

LE MONUMENT A
CLAUDE DEBUSSY

*P*AUL POIRET (left) in 1927. Poiret (1879-1944) had been the great pre-war couturier in the wake of the Ballets Russes, introducing oriental fabrics and colours and in a sense adapting for Parisian fashion what Diaghilev had brought to the stage from 1909 onwards. A precursor of the modern age, he liberated women from corsets but after the war, he attempted to live on his former glory but did not survive the Twenties commercially. He is shown here during the feast day for unmarried women, Saint-Catherine's day.

*T*HE PAINTER Henry Valensi (1883-1960) and his wife at home. Posed in their very
fashionable apartment, she dons a beaded evening dress in a setting that combines Purism
and reminiscences of Poiret. Especially notable for the period are the picture behind
them on the floor, which shows a scene of tennis players, and the one by their heads,
which is a stylized depiction of a ship's deck.

*C*ASSANDRE in his studio, c. 1928 (*above*). Adolphe Mouron, alias Cassandre (1901-1968), was the most famous poster and graphic artist of the Thirties whose style has come to typify the whole era. Especially famous are his posters of ocean liners (see page 184). He is shown here in the studio designed (1924) by Auguste Perret at 11 Rue Albert-Joly at Versailles, which he moved into in 1925. (PHOTO: THÉRÈSE BONNEY)

*P*AOLO FEDERICO GARRETTO, an Italian graphic artist, c.1929/30 (*opposite*). On the banister is an amusing three-dimensional version of the figure on the Nestlé advertisement which he designed. (PHOTO: THÉRÈSE BONNEY)

*A*T THE RACES, a fashion shot (1926) (*above*). Both women are wearing cloche hats and sport a young brittle look. Russian folklore is the theme, replete with the ubiquitous cossack blouse and male shirt collar on top of precipitous high heels. Fur and feather trimmings in the Twenties suffered from a paucity of supplies due to the redrawing of territorial boundaries after the First World War. More conventional furs were in short supply so furriers increasingly looked to Africa and South America, especially chinchilla, which is what the woman on the right may be wearing. On the domestic scene, edible pets were pressed into service for their pelts, especially rabbits which the British coyly referred to as 'Lapin'.

A FASHION SHOT (1925) (*opposite*). Possibly adapted from a more conventional dress which pinpoints the necessity of thrift even in glamorous circles. It was easy to have outfits matched up, a little couturier round the corner could run up any copies of any *Vogue* dresses and a local cobbler would oblige with the accessories. The dress on the right looks like a Delaunay-type *découpage* on a tube dress.

*I*NTERIOR of the perfume shop of Richard Hudnut in the Rue de la Paix, c.1928 (*above*). A rather incredible combination of respectable Napoleon III luxury with an ultra modern façade and window-dressing, designed to simultaneously reassure conservative and adventurous clients. (PHOTO: THÉRÈSE BONNEY)

*S*HOE SHOP of André Pérugia (*opposite*). This Italian shoe-manufacturer was the rival of Salvatore Ferragamo. He designed exclusive lines for couturiers - mainly for Schiaparelli, with whom he produced plastic and fur shoes. The upholstered chair is possibly made from fake snake skin. (PHOTO: THÉRÈSE BONNEY)

*T*HE COUTURIER Paul Poiret with a model (centre) and the writer Colette (1873-1954) in February 1927. Colette, the marvellous author of utterly forgettable novels, briefly (1932-3) ran a beauty parlour specializing in aromatherapy.

*T*HE PHOTOGRAPHER Jacques-Henri Lartigue's first wife Bibi in a Paul Poiret coat, 1922. By now, Poiret's fashions were on the way out. His adherence to his favourite kimono cut in increasingly difficult fabrics, like heavy wools, made him unpopular and Bibi would have found it cumbersome whilst clambering into the sports car. The car racing through the background is a typical feature of Lartigue's shots. (PHOTO: JACQUES-HENRI LARTIGUE)

*C*OCO CHANEL in her business apartment in the Ritz, near her Couture House in the Rue Cambon, 1937. She was famous for her understated clothes and used autobiographical elements as inspiration - *piqué* and alice-bands, for example, came from her childhood orphanage. Some of her lovers helped as well: Grand-Duke Dimitri contributed Russian boots and embroidery and the Duke of Westminster shetland jerseys. (PHOTO: FRANÇOIS KOLLAR)

*S*ALON DE COUTURE of Madame Agnès, c. 1925 (*above*). Fashion shows were still rather intimate events. The clients were ascribed an individual *vendeuse* who would advise them on the suitability of the dresses shown by the models. La Maison Agnes, run by Mme Havet, was a respectable if unadventurous fashion house founded in 1912 and situated on the Rue Auber. In 1930 she became associated with Drecoll, turning the establishment into one of the leading pre-war fashion houses.

*E*LSA SCHIAPARELLI, c.1935 (*opposite*). The Italian fashion designer known as Schiap (1890-1973) is generally presented as the rival of Chanel, but her main contribution was a sense of wit and fun, sadly lacking in other couture houses. She dressed Dalí's wife free in return for ideas, and so she produced the telephone handbag, the pork-chop hat and lip-shaped pockets, all of which have their counterparts in his paintings. (PHOTO: CECIL BEATON)

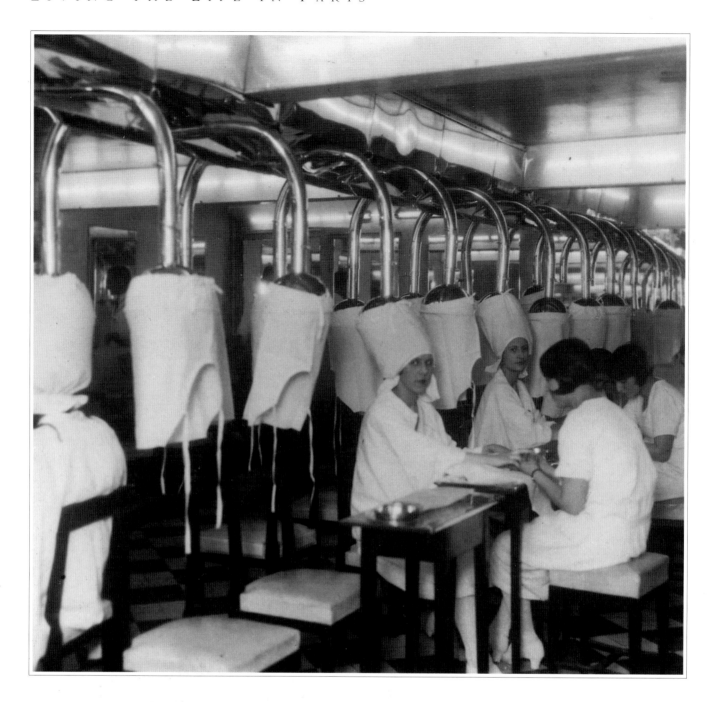

*T*HE ANTOINE SALON, c.1930 (*above*). Having arrived penniless in Paris from Poland in 1901, Antoine quickly became the most famous hairdresser of the age. The extraordinary apparatus for steam- treating the hair, in order to create the ultra-fashionable Marcel wave, gives it a science fiction allure. (PHOTO: THÉRÈSE BONNEY)

*S*ALON DE COIFFURE Lina Cavalieri (*opposite*). The salon appears very classical, and the store street sign is based on wall paintings found at Pompeii. Twenties fashions, and especially the cloche hat, necessitated very short hair and frequent visits to the hairdresser for the structured cropped look. The woman on the left flaunts that most daring innovation of the Twenties, a V-neck in the day-time. (PHOTO: THÉRÈSE BONNEY)

*B*ATHROOM by DIM, c.1928 (*above*). Influenced by Cecil B. De Mille historical extravaganzas, the sunken bath, with gilded mosaic and Aztec patterns, creates a pleasingly decadent quality rather than making bathing an austere necessity. DIM (Décoration Intérieure Moderne) was one of the more avant-garde Art Deco design practices, founded in 1919 by René Joubert. (PHOTO: THÉRÈSE BONNEY)

*B*ATHROOM on display at the Salon d'Automne in 1929 (*opposite*). Designed by Charlotte Perriand (b.1903), Le Corbusier (1887-1965) and his brother Pierre Jeanneret (1896-1967). This ultra-modern ensemble, with smoked glass and chromed steel, is all designed for mass production. The starkness seems appropriate here, yet was essentially just another example of the general 'cleanness' of this aesthetic. (PHOTO: THÉRÈSE BONNEY)

*I*NTERIOR of the Martel brothers villa, c.1930 (*above*). Designed by Mallet-Stevens, Francis Jourdain and Louis Barillet, this shows the influence of the Bauhaus. The weaving has something of a Scandinavian feel to it which adds warmth to a chrome and white starkness that Le Corbusier would have approved of. (PHOTO: THÉRÈSE BONNEY)

*R*OBERT MALLET-STEVENS'S villa, interior, c.1927 (*opposite*). The interior balcony creates a Renaissance feel to the interior, while the tartan on the furniture echoes the patterning on the balustrade, with the best of Twenties elegance. (PHOTO: THÉRÈSE BONNEY)

*E*RTÉ (Romain de Tirtoff, 1892-1990), graphic artist, fashion and costume designer, in his apartment at 124 Rue de Brancas in Sèvres, near Paris, c.1924 (*overleaf*). Born in Saint Petersburg, he moved to Paris before World War I. A youthful prodigy, he worked for Poiret and was under contract to *Harper's Bazaar* from 1916. He designed the most lavish costumes and sets for the French theatre and Hollywood musicals. The black curtains are there to protect art works (which include, on the right maquettes for the Folies Bergère) - he was one of the first artists to retrieve his working drawings for sets and costumes. The studied indolence of the décor, complete with scattered cushions, owes a lot to Poiret. (PHOTO: THÉRÈSE BONNEY)

PERFUME SHOP of Richard Hudnut, built by the architect Jacques Debat-Ponsan, in the Rue de la Paix, c.1928 (*above*). The crystal and mirror perfume fountain was designed by Georges Barbier, famous for his pre-war designs for the *Gazette du Bon Ton*, where such fountains are prominent, and owes its stylistic allegiance to Erté and the Folies Bergère.
(PHOTO: THÉRÈSE BONNEY)

OFFICE DUFET designed by Michel Dufet for the Compagnie Royale Asturienne des Mines, as shown at the Salon of the Société des Artistes Décorateurs in 1930 (*opposite*). The desk was made of zinc. The coordinated approach shows the increasing mania for having each object in an interior visually linked to the next. The innovative Deutscher Werkbund also exhibited at the 1930 Salon, the first time German artists had been officially invited to exhibit in Paris since 1910.

*V*ILLA ALLATINI, 3-5 Rue Mallet Stevens (*above*). One of the villas that Robert Mallet-Stevens built between 1925 and 1927 in a small cul-de-sac in Auteuil that now bears his name. Allatini, the owner of this building, was a filmmaker and there was a screening room for 150 inside. Comprising five villas and six houses in all, the street constitutes one of the most impressive architectural ensembles of the 1920s. Mallet-Stevens was involved in the interior design also and there is a unique harmony in this conception, something which Le Corbusier certainly dreamed of but never had the opportunity to achieve at this time. (PHOTO: THÉRÈSE BONNEY)

*T*OWER on the roof of the home of Joël and Jan Martel by Mallet-Stevens, 10 Rue Mallet-Stevens (*opposite*). Built in white cement and red brick, the tower is reminiscent of a lighthouse or an Indian observatory and shows the architect's extraordinary manipulation of space. (PHOTO: THÉRÈSE BONNEY)

5

INTERNATIONAL EXHIBITIONS

IT'S SUCH FUN, the Eiffel Tower's off for a spin
Like a loony she leaps, feet joined, over the Seine
CHARLES TRENET: *Y'A DE LA JOIE* (1937)

IN THE INTERWAR YEARS, three international exhibitions were organized to display the civilising forces of France and each one has come to typify significant aspects of its period. The distance travelled from the 1925 Arts Décoratifs Exhibition to the 1937 Exhibition is revealing of the way some symptomatic detailing had grown into portentous symbolism.

Every epoch has its style and its signature-tune. Paris in the Twenties and, to a certain extent, during the whole of the inter-war period swanked in Art Deco. The style really started around 1910 (with the *Gazette du Bon Ton*) and reached its apotheosis at the 1925 Exposition des Arts Décoratifs. Its jumble of Art Nouveau sinuosity, Ballets Russes gaudiness and Cubist angularity have come to symbolize design for the whole period. Female figures with swan necks inspired by Modigliani are the nymphs and goddesses of the Twenties, found on lamp stands, clocks, fashion drawings in *Jardin des Modes* and *Vogue.* With the help of designers like Chanel, women endowed with rather boyish figures even managed to look like the idealized prototype, at least on photographs!

An extraordinary outburst of creativity shook every aspect of design from furniture to bookbinding, unified by an overarching sense of modernity. There is a kind of perfection to Art Deco which all came together in the most successful building of the exhibition, the Hôtel d'un Collectionneur, an adaptation of the house Patout had built for Ruhlmann. It had some of the best furniture Ruhlmann had ever designed and was set in an ideal sculpture garden. The flowing quality of Art Deco is closer to the eighteenth century, which was a considerable influence, especially in its earlier phase. It is also comfortably bourgeois in comparison to what was being produced by the Bauhaus in Germany, which is why it has come to typify the epoch so strongly. The 1925 Exhibition encompassed many things, but perhaps above all, it was about defining a style that was also a way of life in a modern society beyond wars and revolution. It was as if one were trying to symbolize an ideal future, which was naïvely reassuring and child-like, even in its political outlook: Germany was not allowed to

*T*HE HÔTEL DU COLLECTION-NEUR, 1925. Architecture by Pierre Patout, exterior detail by Joseph Janniot, low relief by Joseph Bernard. The interior was designed by Jacques-Emile Ruhlmann (1879-1933) who was acclaimed as the Riesener of his time and produced the most prestigious furniture since the time of Louis XVI. Patout was famous for his ocean liner style, which was very influential in the Thirties.

participate, something which would be impossible in the next great Exhibition even with the threat of World War looming large.

Buildings were constructed in styles that avoided any conventional stylistic reference, even though the sheer monumentality may have been an indication of monolithic political tendencies being put in place. It was as if history were something artists and designers had to supersede. With hindsight, Patout's monumental entrance on the Place de la Concorde side, with its ten stark pylons dwarfing passers-by, looks forward to the more sinister aspects of the 1937 Exhibition.

The site of the 1925 Exhibition was the same as the 1900 Exhibition and the future 1937 one, spanning the Esplanade des Invalides and the areas opposite on the right bank around the Trocadéro, the future site of the Palais de Chaillot. Everything was built round the existing fountains and trees, and the buildings were low temporary structures made of wood and plaster dusted with gold and silver powder. Metal was only used for a decorative effect or in conjunction with glass as in Lalique's obelisk fountain, lit from the inside. On the Alexandre III bridge, a row of luxurious boutiques were built and floating restaurants named 'Amour', 'Délices' and 'Orgues', decorated by Poiret and Raoul Dufy cruised up and down the Seine.

GENERAL view of the main axis of the 1925 Arts Décoratifs exhibition on a Whitsun bank-holiday. In the foreground is 'Studium Louvre', the pavilion of the Grand Magasins du Louvre. Further down is 'Primavera', the pavilion of the Printemps store, while opposite it is the Pavillon Pomone, the pavilion of the Bon Marché store. Unlike most of the other pavilions, those of the four large department stores (that of the Galeries Lafayette is further to the right) tried to offer well designed but largely mass-produced articles.

THE MONUMENTAL Porte d' Honneur entrance to the 1925 Exhibition, by the Grand Palais. The structure was designed by Henri Favier and André Ventre, with wrought iron work by Edgar Brandt, glass work by Lalique and sculpture by Navarre. The obelisks here refer to the one dominating the nearby Place de Concorde and symbolize the historic significance of the event. The exhibition had been inaugurated on the 28 April 1925 by President Doumergue and no less than 4000 of his favoured guests.

The exhibition had been talked about since 1912 with a view to it taking place in 1915, but it was delayed by the war until 1925. Twenty nations participated in addition to France and the exhibition was intended as a showcase for the latest in design. One of the general stipulations for entry stated: 'Works admitted to the exhibition must be those of modern inspiration and of genuine originality, executed by artists, artisans, manufacturers, model makers and publishers, in keeping with the demands of modern decoration and industrial art'. Exhibits were also required to fulfill a particular need or function. Any imitation of a past style was strictly forbidden. As a consequence countries aspired to produce a maximum of novelty and a minimum of tradition, which paradoxically led to a certain uniformity. Oddly, the Americans declined their invitation to exhibit on the grounds that there was no modern art in the country. This thirst for modernity meant that the three barges decorated by Poiret and Dufy bankrupted Poiret but held little attraction for visitors, who thought such opulence *passé*.

Le Corbusier's Pavillon de l'Esprit Nouveau, replete with paintings by Juan Gris, Léger, Jeanneret (Le Corbusier's real name) and Ozenfant must have seemed minimalist in contrast with others. It was a summary of Le Corbusier's principles, with its unbounded faith in the machine aesthetic

153

and natural order, a microcosm of his ideal habitat, destined for mass reproduction but probably lost on the general public. Wary of endorsing anything too radical, until the opening the pavilion was hidden behind a fence six metres high. In addition it was given one of the worst sites. It was conceived as a showcase for Le Corbusier's ideas about town planning and included two model exhibits: the 'Voisin' plan for Paris and the panorama of a contemporary city for 3,000,000 inhabitants. The former which would have involved building a series of tower blocks in a wide stretch just to the north of the Louvre was sponsored by the Voisin car firm (Citroën, by contrast, was responsible for the 200,000 lights that adorned the Eiffel Tower and advertised its company name). Le Corbusier claimed 'The motor car has killed the great city. The motor car must save the great city'. His plan made what he described as a 'frontal attack on the most diseased quarters of the city and the narrowest streets'. Needless to say it was never even considered by the authorities.

Most visitors were more interested in sumptuous displays such as Ruhlmann's Hôtel du Collectionneur or those set up by the large department stores. One of the largest projects was the Ambassade Française, an ideal embassy with twenty-five rooms planned by different designers: the large reception hall was created by Robert Mallet-Stevens and had paintings by Robert Delaunay and Léger. Mallet-Stevens was also responsible for the Pavilion of Tourism, while Perret designed the official theatre building. Of the foreign entries the most striking, and modern, was the Soviet pavilion by Constantin Melnikov, which had a Worker's Club by Rodchenko. Yet the general emphasis on bourgeois luxury, which irritated some critics, was a deliberate attempt to assert France's primacy in this area, especially in response to avant-garde German design. The only contribution from Germany was Peter Behrens' tearoom for the Austrian pavilion, which was allowed only because the architect was then teaching at the Vienna Academy of Fine Arts. Some had claimed that the exclusion of Germany was more from fear of competition than because of the residual wounds of war. Predictably, the Surrealists dismissed the whole exhibition as 'a huge joke'.

The Exhibition Internationale Coloniale of 1931 took place in the Parisian suburb of Vincennes and was organised by Maréchal Lyautey, one of France's foremost military colonial figures, and Paul Reynaud the

*A*GNÈS RITTENER, a hat designer (1919-49) called Madame Agnès, at the Pavillon de la Mode, Arts Décoratifs exhibition, 1925. She is wearing a typical dressing-gown-cut dress with a geometric hand- painted design, by Jean Dunand, and is seen posing doefully in front a lacquerwork screen entitled *Rencontres*, also by Dunand. The Swiss-born Dunand (1877-1942) was famed for his metal- and lacquerwork.
(PHOTO: THÉRÈSE BONNEY)

colonial minister. The previous year there had been a centenary exhibition celebrating the conquest of Algeria at the Petit Palais, while in 1922 there was a colonial exhibition in Marseille. In part, the 1931 exhibition was staged as a response to the British Empire Exhibition of 1924-5 at Wembley in England. The fact that Britain, after much bickering, decided not to attend conveniently left France as the most important imperial power at the exhibition. Among the other nations that exhibited were Italy, Portugal, Holland, Denmark, Belgium and America, some of whom could scarcely even claim to have an empire. Denmark displayed Greenland as its empire, while Italy harked back to its imperial Roman past. Mindful of the great success of Art Deco at the 1925 Exhibition, the organizers of the 1931 event tried to encourage the creation of a 'Colonial style' to supersede it and various designers thus had displays showing the obvious influence of decorative African and other forms.

Attracted by the slogan 'See the world in a day!', over eight million visitors filed past to admire the accomplishments of colonialism, presented as humane and generous (as opposed to other colonising countries such as Great Britain or Germany). Date and palm trees were specially planted to create the atmosphere of far off lands. Tribesmen were 'imported' for the occasion and there were boulevards lined with monumental, inflated

*T*HE TEMPLE OF ANGKOR WAT, reconstructed for the 1931 Exposition Coloniale. The original (in what is now Cambodia) was certainly influential in design of the later Twenties. In fact, many of the more exotic elements in fashion and accessories in the Thirties can be traced back to the 1931 Exhibition.

RENÉE PERLE in Lartigue's car at the Exposition Coloniale, 1931. In the background can be seen a 'Golf Bar' built in 'African style'. Fashion designers were increasingly looking toward Africa to provide novelty skins such as zebra, giraffe, monkey furs and various ostrich products.
(PHOTO: JACQUES-HENRI LARTIGUE)

recreations of African huts or Indochinese temples (including a colossal reconstruction of the Temple of Angkor Wat). The public sampled exotic food, heard strange music, admired mosques and temples, and saw endearing little suntanned dancers, who were made to feel grateful that France was, in fact, saving them in exchange for rice, cocoa and bananas. This ideology was further reinforced in school and in hopelessly romantic films such as *Le Grand Jeu* or escapist novels by Pierre Mac Orlan. Edith Piaf sang *Mon Légionnaire*, and cohorts of damsels moped at the thought of soldiers smelling sweetly of hot sand and palm trees. Those far-away colonies provided the stuff of dreams in many an *Habitation à Bon Marché*. The interest in the colonies at this time stimulated travel, leading to the construction of huge luxury liners decked out in the style of their destination country – the *Normandie*, built in 1935, was the most sumptuous of its day and was filled with luxurious and elaborate interiors.

Reynaud and Lyautey wrote: 'Millions and millions of Frenchmen have visited the splendours of Vincennes. Our colonies are for them no longer unknown names. They know of their grandeur, their beauty, their resources. Each one of them feels himself to be the citizen of "La Plus Grande France", the France of the five continents of the world'. Having recovered Alsace Lorraine after the war, France could comfortably look further afield.

In addition, during the Depression, the colonies became of tremendous economic importance, representing a huge source of cheap raw materials as well as a large market for French goods. The deal was very much one way, as was illustrated by the Palais de la Section Métropolitaine, the severe and menacing pavilion of the mother country, which had a huge tower 85 metres high. Inside it, the two offices of Reynaud and Lyautey were adorned with frescoes extolling the value of the colonies to France: 'The Contribution of the East to the West' and 'The Contribution of Africa to the West'. The only permanent remnant of the exhibition was the Musée des Colonies which had a frieze running around its walls entitled 'The Colonies' Contribution to France'. Among its panoply of symbolic female figures, only Equality was notably absent.

The Exhibition was the supreme exercise in colonialist propaganda, possibly a last shot, aimed at uniting all French citizens, not just the army and missionaries, behind a victorious Imperial France that purportedly brought civilisation to the savages. This somewhat dubious ideal was presented as a panacea to all that was ailing *la Patrie*, even though France failed to provide its much vaunted liberty, equality and fraternity to the colonies. From Indochina to North Africa, nationalism and discontent were growing steadily.

The odd thing is that the Left did not criticize the tenets of colonialism any more than the Right, the differences were about the degree of altruistic attitude and involvement. The Communists had initially been totally against Colonialism, but under the left-wing coalition, the Popular Front, their thinking shifted. In fact only a few intellectuals – especially the Surrealists – spoke up violently against the exhibition and consistently opposed its underlying principles, in the name of native culture. The Surrealists issued two pamphlets, the first one, 'Ne Visitez pas l'Exposition Coloniale', called for a total boycott of the event and protested against the 'colonialist banditry' it represented. It was claimed that its sole purpose was to give 'to the citizens of metropolitan France the feeling of being proprietors . . . so they can hear the distant sounds of gunfire without flinching'. Their second attack came after the Dutch East Indies Pavilion had burnt down: 'This is the work of colonization completed, which began by massacres and was continued by forced conversions, slave labour and diseases'.

PARC DES ATTRACTIONS in the Exposition Internationale des Arts et Techniques of 1937. This Disneyland amusement park, with its reconstructions of medieval French buildings (some notably in Alsatian style), was a popular part of the show and gives an idea of the vast amount of money spent on the exhibition, money that France could ill afford.

The Exposition Internationale des Arts et Techniques dans la Vie Moderne of 1937 revealed political troubles much closer to home. Léon Blum, the leader of the Popular Front, attempted to convince the 25,000 workers involved with it that to finish on time would be a proletarian victory against international Fascism. They were not convinced and the show opened nearly a month after the scheduled Labour day inauguration, with only five pavilions ready: Germany, Russia, Italy, Denmark and Holland. The others continued to be opened until August. Thirty-four million visitors poured in from all over the world, despite the expense and the frequent discomfort. Hotels refused group rates, train fares increased, taxis went on strike, as did waiters and chambermaids, but perhaps this was what people expected of Paris.

Attracting around six times as many visitors as the 1925 Exhibition and covering an incomparably larger area, the 1937 Exhibition expressed the tensions of the period, while attempting to make from them some sort of harmonious whole. The most striking and symbolic image the visitor had on entering was the sight of the German and Soviet pavilions looming opposite each other across the Champ de Mars. The Nazi pavilion, 54 metres high, had a huge eagle at its top, while the Soviet building was crowned by an enormous 33 metre high statue of an 'industrial worker and

a collective farm girl' holding a hammer and sickle. Albert Speer, the architect of the German pavilion, claimed that he had stumbled across Boris Yofan's plans for the Soviet building in the early stages of design and deliberately planned the German building as a response to it. In both cases, the official architecture on show here was light-years away from the real innovations each country had produced in the previous decade, with the Bauhaus and Constructivism. The German catalogue for the exhibition spoke of its contribution in ominous terms: 'The fact that certain elements in these buildings are reminiscent of antique forms is not the result of mere slavish copying. The explanation may perhaps be found in an attitude towards life and its problems which resembles that of the Ancient World. We no longer deny the things of this earth in fear, we train our people to be strong in spirit and in body'. A similar neo-classical style, with the same connotations, was used for the Italian pavilion. Yet it was also the basic style of the two permanent buildings constructed for the exhibition: the Palais de Chaillot and the Palais de Tokyo.

The proposed theme of the exhibition was the marriage of art and science in the service of the modern world. Consequently, there were pavilions dedicated to radio, aeronautics, electricity and light, discovery and so on. Artists were to provide the decorations for all these buildings and a

MUSÉE D'ART MODERNE, Palais de Tokyo, 1937. Reviewing the design of this new building (comprising the City and State modern art museums), the critic Jean Favier wrote in *La Construction Moderne* on February 1935 'It is with a real satisfaction that we note that that cubist fanatics, in the shape of those recently imported architects, will not be allowed to soil with their rantings an event designed to bring out the supremacy of French art'. The choice of neo-classicism, so much in favour in Rome and Berlin, was a way of rejecting modern architecture. The inaugural exhibition here was in fact a retrospective of French art from the fourteenth to the nineteenth centuries - the modern art exhibitions were put elsewhere.

RAOUL DUFY painting *La Fée Electricité* ('The Electricity Fairy') at Saint-Ouen near Paris with the American photographer Thérèse Bonney. The huge mural (600 m² on 250 panels - purportedly the world's biggest picture) was installed in the Palace of Light and Electricity, designed by Robert Mallet-Stevens, at the 1937 Exhibition. The theme was the origin of electrical energy, set in a fairy Olympus complete with wheatfields and laboursaving devices. The work of the versatile and prolific Bonney was driven by her immense curiosity for every aspect of French life.
(PHOTO: THÉRÈSE BONNEY)

total of 500 painters and nearly 300 sculptors were employed as well as hundreds of other decorative artists: unemployment had hit artists as much as anybody else. For the Pavilion of Electricity and Light, Dufy produced an enormous painted panel some 10 metres by 60 metres entitled *The Electricity Fairy*. The Light and Art Studio around Robert Delaunay and Félix Aublet produced huge decorative panels for the Pavilion of the Air, which included his characteristic coloured discs, symbolic of light itself. Light proved an oddly prevalent, symbolic feature of the exhibition: from the top of the pavilion light beams shot into the night sky, conquering the air, while those that shone between the German and Soviet buildings seemed like an exchange of fire. The Eiffel Tower itself, an irritatingly old monument for the modern age, was dolled up in 8km of fluorescent tubes.

The Spanish pavilion reminded the world of the ongoing tragedy of the Civil War while visitors were swilling beer and lemonade from one exhibit to the next. Picasso had been commissioned to paint a mural and was free to choose the theme. On 26 April, four days before the official opening date of the Exhibition, the small Basque town of Guernica was destroyed through the joint action of Spanish rebels and their Nazi German allies. Some 1654 people were killed, mainly civilians. Picasso had three photographs from the May 1st issue of *Paris Soir* to go from and produced

the most poignant work in the Exhibition. Aside from a few young artists and those who were genuinely upset by the Spanish tragedy, to most visitors this was just another exhibit, only a bit more peculiar than the others because it was a modern art-work and therefore incomprehensible. In Picasso's work the optimism about technology and science found elsewhere was turned to dust: technology was here presented as an evil monster not an endearing fairy. At the top of the painting an electric light bulb fixes the scene of terror in black and white, like a photograph.

The irony of this rude intrusion of reality into the artificial world of the exhibition was made all the more savage by the existence of a pavilion and tower of peace at one of the central points of the site. Thrown in as a hasty afterthought, the pavilion was not inaugurated until after the exhibition had opened. An exhibit inside the pavilion used a clock to illustrate the horrors of the previous world war, reminding visitors that for every minute of its duration four soldiers were killed and nine injured. Doubtless to many this was thought to be just a recitation of the past, not an augury of the future. Yet barely three years later Hitler would be reviewing Paris.

SPANISH PAVILION (designed by José Luis Sert) at the 1937 Exhibition with Alexander Calder's *Mercury Fountain* in the foreground and Picasso's *Guernica* behind. Unlike many of the exhibits elsewhere, the political statements here were created through spectacular avant-garde art works, of which Picasso's *Guernica* was the most famous. Calder's rather playful work, using mercury from Almadén, fascinated the visitors who liked throwing coins into it to watch them float.

(PHOTO: THÉRÈSE BONNEY)

*A*SCULPTURE entitled *Les Hommes Machines* on show at the 1925 Exposition des Arts
Décoratifs. Beneath the title, the label bears the comment 'Pour ouvrir les têtes
passéistes' ('To open the minds of the backward-looking'). This attitude reflects the
contemporary fascination for machines. The idea of man as being a kind of machine had,
in fact, been current in avant-garde circles since before the war. Though the figures here
have been given smiling faces, the mechanized, impersonal aura is nevertheless sinister.

THE GALERIE DES BOUTIQUES by Henri Sauvage, with sculptures by Raynaud and decoration by Cottineau, 1925 Arts Décoratifs exhibition (*above*). The barbaric splendour of this building draws on a variety of confused exotic influences, including the colonies, tales of exploration, Poiret salon exoticism and, last but not least, Hollywood films.

THE PORTE D'ORSAY, one of the main entrances to the 1925 Arts Décoratifs exhibition, designed by Louis Boileau (*opposite*). The exhibition was open for fifteen hours a day, from 10.00am to 1.00am, as seen on one of the signs here. Typography is here the dominant visual element: indeed lettering was a major part of Art Deco design on paper, fabric and neon, and has come to symbolize the whole era.

*B*IBI, Lartigue's wife, at the 1925 Arts Décoratifs exhibition with friends. The exhibition stretched from the esplanade of the Invalides to the Pont Alexandre III, which was lined with fashion and souvenir boutiques, and also included the space in front of the Petit and Grand Palais. This mammoth area provided varied if exhausting entertainment for the French and international visitors who travelled far and wide to admire the show.
(PHOTO: JACQUES-HENRI LARTIGUE)

*T*HE REFRESHMENTS stand at the 1925 Exhibition selling ice-lollies
(in French these are called *esquimaux* - eskimoes). An exciting treat at a
time when refrigerators were the exception rather than the rule.

THE PAVILLON DE L'ESPRIT NOUVEAU by Le Corbusier, at the 1925 Exhibition (*opposite, below*). Comprising a single unit that could be stacked and multiplied as required, this was one of the most innovative pavilions in the whole exhibition. The international jury of the exhibition wanted to award it first prize but was prevented by the French Academicians using their power of veto. Nevertheless, the French President of the international jury, Auguste Perret, exclaimed: 'It's idiotic, it doesn't even hold up, there isn't any architecture to it.'

THE RUSSIAN PAVILION at the 1925 Exhibition (*above*). This Constructivist pavilion, designed by Constantin Melnikov, was the most avant-garde on show and was the subject of heated arguments in Paris. The steep staircase was particularly decried, J. Hiriart's contemptuous remarks in *Les Arts Décoratifs Modernes* were typical: 'Russia destroys everything achieving only an uncomfortable staircase, a glass cage where only emptiness and disorder are perceptible'.

INTERIOR of the Pavillon de l'Esprit Nouveau by Le Corbusier and Amédée Ozenfant at the 1925 Exhibition (*opposite, above*). The painting furthest right is by Le Corbusier himself (as Jeanneret), while that next to it is by Léger. The building was a summary of Purist principles, but was largely lost on the general public who thought it too minimalist. All the furniture was supposed to be mass-produced, but some items had to be custom built to factory prototypes as they would not fit through the 'standard' doors.

DISPLAY by Edgar Brandt, the architect Henri Favier and other designers in La Salle des Ambassadeurs at the 1925 Exhibition (*above*). Brandt (1880-1960) was one of the most famous and influential metalworkers of the time. On the right is his screen *L'Oasis* made of iron, brass, copper and other patinated metals, described by one contemporary critic as a kind of large jewellery. The whole luxurious ensemble is archetypally Art Deco.

STAND in the Pavillon Fontaine et Compagnie, 1925 Exhibition (*below left*). The printed fabrics are by the Société Alsacienne de Blanc et d'Impression and others and are typical of such Alsatian mass-produced textiles.

INTERIOR of the Parfumerie Française at the 1925 Exhibition, designed by Raguenet and Maillard, complete with a glass fountain (by Lalique) as was frequent in perfume stores (*opposite*). The setting is a tent-like structure recalling Sheherezade. Fashion and luxury industries were an important part of the Exhibition, as if to reinstate the glory of victorious France to a self-congratulating public and foreign buyers.

*P*AVILION of French West Africa,
1931 Colonial Exhibition (*above*).
The best aspect of the exhibition
was that the public discovered the
reality of African architecture and
civilization beyond a few artefacts
on patronizing display. The great
American art connoisseur Peggy
Guggenheim was bowled over by
what she saw and began to collect
African art.

*T*HE CENTRE DES COLONIES at the
International Exhibition of 1937
(*right*). Though nowhere near as
large a feature as in 1931, the
colonies were again represented in
1937. However, because of their
traditional architecture, most
were relegated to the margins of
the site. Shown here is the French
Equatorial Africa exhibit by the
architects Auguste Biaggi and J.
G. Lambert.

*T*UNISIAN PAVILION, complete with a Tunisian street, a reproduction of the Sidi Ben Zaid minaret in Tunis and a bazaar, Colonial Exhibition, 1931 (*above*). North Africa was beginning to attract adventurous intellectuals seeking exotica. During the year of the exhibition Saint-Exupéry's *Vol de Nuit* ('Night Flight') was published, followed shortly by the Guerlain perfume of the same name.

*I*NAUGURATION of the Pavilion of French West Africa, Colonial Exhibition, 1931 (*left*). Bedouins stampeding past on camels, Vietnamese musicians, Arab belly dancers all brought a taste of the exotic to visitors who mostly had never been abroad.

173

GENERAL view of the International
Exhibition of 1937 from the
Palais de Chaillot. On the left of
the Eiffel Tower is the German
pavilion and opposite it the Soviet
one. The enormous scale of these
buildings not only dwarfed the
crowds of visitors, but also the
other national pavilions: just
down from the Soviet building,
on the other side of the bridge,
can be seen the pavilion erected by
Great Britain.

*A*DVERTISING section of the 1937 Exhibition, with the Column of Peace in the distance (*above*). Graphics and advertising were an important aspect of the exhibition and reflected the steady growth of the consumer industry in the inter-war years.
(PHOTO: THÉRÈSE BONNEY)

L'HOMME by Pierre Traverse in the gardens of the Trocadéro at the 1937 Exhibition (*opposite*). The Exhibition was to be the Popular Front's tribute to France as a democracy: this figure, reviewing the scene, may also symbolize (French) humanity hopefully triumphing over imminent disaster before teetering off its pedestal.
(PHOTO: THÉRÈSE BONNEY)

*G*ENERAL view of the 1937 Exhibition as seen from Eiffel Tower (*overleaf*). In the background are the two huge wings of the newly built Palais de Chaillot, between which is the bronze Tower of Peace, modelled on Trajan's Column in Rome, with the Pavilion of Peace round its base.

*P*AVILLON DE L'UNION DES ARTISTES MODERNES, main exhibition hall, 1937 Exhibition (*above*). The mural on the left, *Accompaniment of Architecture*, is by Fernand Léger, Albert Gleizes and Leopold Survage, while the furniture is by Jean Prouvé. This pavilion was one of the most luminous in the whole venture. The architect Georges-Henri Pingusson designed a sheet glass and metal structure which ideally brought out the qualities of the works presented. The UAM was an association of artists, architects and designers founded in 1929, which aimed to encourage modern art and ideas.
(PHOTO: THÉRÈSE BONNEY)

*P*AVILLON PHOTO-CINÉ-PHONO, 1937 Exhibition (*opposite*). This particularly popular exhibit, designed by Saint-Maurice and Lemaire, complete with three-dimensional film as a frieze was placed just under the Eiffel Tower. It shows not only the triumph of movies and film over live entertainment, but also extolls the technological innovations of the age. There were no less than 40 other cinema screens in the exhibition. (PHOTO THÉRÈSE BONNEY)

PAVILLION DE L'AIR at the 1937 Exhibition. The décor of the exhibition was orchestrated by the Light and Art Studio around Robert Delaunay and Félix Aublet, who were required to hire 50 out-of-work artists. The main hall is like a giant cockpit with suspended aeroplanes linked by gangways on which visitors could climb on.

THE TOURISM PAVILLION at the 1937 Exhibition (*above*). The deck chairs and posters - especially Cassandre's most renowned posters for the *Normandie* liner - suggest travel and escapism. Another section of the pavillion was devoted to the newly nationalized railways and the top floor ceiling was covered with huge photographs of French landmarks, each 35m high. Tourism was the rallying point for the international visitors to the show, hence the importance given to this pavillion, which was designed by Pierre Sardou.

THE PAVILION OF ELEGANCE at the 1937 Exhibition (*opposite, above*). Certainly one of the most lauded exhibits, designed by Emile Aillaud, Etienne Kohlmann and André Ventre. This is the Haute Couture room, with evening dresses by Madeleine Vionnet in the front and perfume stands on the side put together in a Surrealist inspired setting. The building was covered with blue porcelain in honour of Jeanne Lanvin, the president of this section whose favourite colour it was. Just next door stood the Club des Oiseaux, the most elegant restaurant of the Exhibition, where a select few who could afford the Haute Couture on show came to dine.

FURNITURE by Jean Prouvé in the main exhibition hall of the Pavillon de l'Union des Artistes Modernes, 1937 Exhibition (*opposite, below*). Made from industrially produced components of plexiglass and perforated steel, this use of new materials and techniques was a paradigm of modernity. The languor of the Thirties silhouette is ideally suited to this type of chair, ideal for quaffing cocktails and easy to keep clean in a world where domestics were getting scarce. (PHOTO: THÉRÈSE BONNEY)

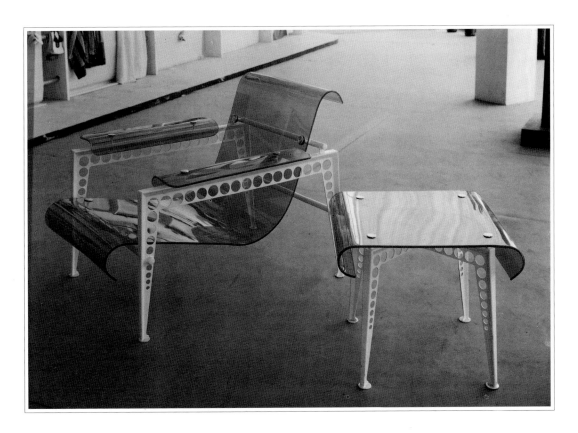

6

THE PORTENTOUS
THIRTIES

PARIS IS COLD Paris is hungry
Paris no longer eats chestnuts in the streets
Paris has put on old women's clothes
Paris sleeps standing without air in the Métro
PAUL ELUARD, 'COURAGE', 1942

STREET SCENE during the government of the Popular Front, 19 September 1936. People of opposed political affiliations are simultaneously putting up a poster and pulling it down. Despite the establishment in May 1936 of the Popular Front, a loose union of Socialists, Communists and Radicals led by Léon Blum, strikes and general unrest continued. Blum valiantly tried to improve social and work conditions (including a month's holiday with pay), nationalized the trains and the Bank of France, controlled prices of grain but because of reticent economic policies, prices (already the highest in the West) shot up faster than wages and crisis ensued.

IN THE THIRTIES, there was an unprecedented degree of political awareness among young intellectuals. Active involvement (what the French call *engagement*) was deemed essential: one had to be militant about every issue and to sport one's opinions in every possible way, from everyday behaviour – including clothing (red scarves for Communists, brown shirts for National Socialists, black shirts for Italian Fascists etc.) – to planning insurrections and writing manifestoes. In brief it meant pursuing causes worth dying for, at least in Spain, or if not in the daily demonstrations, sit-ins or riots that characterized the decade. Countless magazines were published, many of which had distinguished contributors, writers and polemicists. Thus Robert Brasillach wrote in *Réaction* as well as in the gutter press, namely the odiously anti-Semitic *Je Suis Partout*. On the other extreme, the Association of Revolutionary Writers and Artists (the AEAR) published *Commune*, with articles by Henri Barbusse, Gide, Giono and Malraux. Between the two, many others flourished, including the liberal Catholic *Esprit* and Breton's *Le Surréalisme au service de la revolution*. The Surrealists were Communist militants, the degree of involvement causing rifts between the members. And on the outer fringes were countless sub-groups with their own publications. Many adolescents went around collecting funds from weary relatives to start short-lived militant poetic magazines with fancy names like *L'Ours en Peluche* ('The Teddy-bear') or *L'Oeuf dur* ('The Hard-boiled Egg'). Only one or two issues came out, the publishers went broke and the aspiring revolutionaries then proceeded to start another magazine. The main thing was to make one's mark in these troubled times.

Politics had been seeping into the arts since the Twenties. Already in 1923, the first meeting of the P.E.N. Club posed the question of the role of intellectuals in creating a new world order. From the later 1920s this was one of the main preoccupations of intellectuals like Breton and especially

SALVADOR DALÍ in his appartment in the Rue de l'Université in 1939. Just before the fall of France in June 1940, Salvador Dalí (1904-89) emigrated to New York with Gala in a state of political confusion. It was partly his sense of provocation that made him support Franco, much to the disgust of his former Surrealist friends, who were mostly Communists.
(PHOTO: SERGE LIDO)

future Communist militants such as Aragon and Eluard. Drieu La Rochelle, Brasillach and Céline opted for Fascism, out of despair and conviction. The Surrealists initially chose Communism on aesthetic more than moral grounds: as likely as not, they could not abide those straight-laced Action Française supporters and variegated Mussolini sympathisers, which included Futurists with Dada-style views close to their own. It was partly out of a sense of provocation that Dalí went overboard for Franco as well as having an early fascination for Hitler. Léger and his entourage expressed their franker sympathies for Moscow, but for reasons more structured than the Surrealists' unconditional allegiance to subversion.

In the Thirties the lot of the avant-garde, as for many others, worsened. Artists lived through hard times in the Depression, as there were no institutions ready to buy contemporary works. They had to depend on collectors, but these too were broke and at best unadventurous. So many artists could not afford paint and canvas and had to rely on haphazard charity. In 1935 there was a place where they could exchange their works for basic commodities or else they could go to a canteen for needy intellectuals, one like that which the painter Marie Wassilieff had run in the First World War. This brute material fact doubtless heightened political awareness.

One might have expected the avant-garde of the Thirties to have opened up people's minds to new ways of considering the world. Yet most of them still fell about with laughter when they looked at Picasso, sniggered in front of the Surrealists and hooted at Satie. The much-hallowed avant-garde was, in the years it was created, a minuscule fringe movement with a tiny handful of spectators. To live in anything designed by Le Corbusier was a nightmarish proposition and to envisage commissioning modernist architects to design any kind of official building was totally unimaginable. Public building styles were in some kind of generic monumental neo-classicism, ideally adapted to imperial and totalitarian aspirations of the epoch. The best example was the Musée d'Art Moderne in the Palais de Tokyo, one of the few permanent remnants of the 1937 Exhibition, of which Hitler said it was his favourite building in Paris. Likewise, while the Thirties experienced an extraordinary poetic surge, it was works such as Gabriel Chevallier's *Clochemerle* saga and Simenon's Maigret series that were the best-sellers of the decade.

For artists, it was technically more difficult to make political statements if one wanted to go beyond realistic representation. Hence the absence of any real innovation in the Thirties, which left the field to Socialist Realism and its Nazi version in Germany. Only Picasso and a few other artists like Miró and Masson, influenced by a Surrealist notion of freedom, evolved a kind of visual aggression and anti-aesthetic language. In Picasso's work, this is particularly evident in the works that followed *Guernica*. Nevertheless, despite the constant talk of art for the people, the sad truth is that neither Picasso, nor Edouard Pignon, nor Léger, nor the many other committed left-wing artists, ever reached the workers, who hardly got a chance to see modern art. Even if they had, it is doubtful that they would have responded to it at that time. Yet these artists, who were well aware of their limitations, chose deliberately not to pander to a form of acceptable realism, which was rampant from Moscow to Berlin, or decorative sentimentality of the type on show in most Parisian Salons. This in itself was a political statement.

In retrospect, even some of the avant-garde theories had a disconcerting affinity with the darker political developments of this period. Attitudes towards machinery, technology, sport, architecture and human rights seem

horribly coherent in the context of rising totalitarian ideologies. For example, Le Corbusier initially planned his ideal city as an élitist, centralized structure with factories and garden cities for the working class situated outside some kind of security-zone, a machine on a vast scale. At the time, he could not have been aware to what extent this could be amalgamated into totalitarian ideologies, in which individuality was submerged like a cog within a well-oiled machine, or like a uniformed gymnast in one of the many parades so characteristic of the Thirties.

Much of what came to the fore in the Thirties had been lurking ominously in the background in the Twenties, in the arts as elsewhere. Nationalism and xenophobia may at first have seemed an unfortunate but understandable part of post-war readjustment but their consequences were soon amplified and polarized in the Thirties. In this anxious atmosphere art was thought a tremendous threat to society: the right-wing thugs who interrupted the screening of *L'Age d'Or* were not upset by its radical

EVERY YEAR, on the second Sunday in May, there was a festival in honour of Joan of Arc, which was centred around the statue of her in the Place des Pyramides. Here, on 11 May 1936, Colonel François de la Roque leads a parade of the Croix de Feu through the Place des Pyramides down the Rue de Rivoli. The Croix de Feu was the most important extreme right-wing group of the period and was founded by de la Roque, an aristocratic war veteran, who lacked charismatic appeal but was a skilful organizer.

MUSICIANS singing in the Place de la Madeleine to raise money for the unemployed. Sometimes well-known artists would join in as well to express their solidarity and some were seen in the frequent demonstrations of the period. Street level protest of every kind has always been of paramount importance in France.

aesthetics but rather its attack on establishment values. Shouting 'Death to the Jews!' as they wrecked both the cinema and the exhibits, they also publicly protested against the 'immorality of this Bolshevist spectacle' and the film was subsequently banned.

The 'Aragon Affair' of 1931-2 became a focal point for the politicization of the arts. By 1930 the poet Aragon had virtually split with the Surrealists in favour of Communism, causing much acrimony, and in 1931 he wrote a short poem called 'Front rouge' which included such lines as 'Shoot Léon Blum . . . Shoot the trained bears of social democracy'. In 1932 remaining copies of the journal that had published the poem were seized by the police, and Aragon was arrested and charged with incitement to murder and with provoking insubordination in the army. The penalty could have been five years in gaol. Despite having rejected them, the Surrealists organized a petition in his defence, which was signed by famous artists all over Europe, including Braque, Picasso, Matisse, Brecht, Mann, Le Corbusier and Lorca. The fact that the poem was bad mattered little to the sense of vulnerability such cases generated, forcing artists to unite and defend themselves as never before.

Just about everyone born between 1890 and 1910 had his or her solution to the impotence of the system and the hypocrisy of the ruling parties. The

humanist ideal inherited by the socialist and radical traditions was now defunct. Even the far right, rather than choose allegiance to royalist views, aspired to a new order that would overturn the existing one: perhaps this is why so many of them were lapsed Communists who needed some kind of mythical justification to their beliefs. Dreams of a nebulous, albeit muscular, golden age certainly inspired writers like Drieu la Rochelle and politicians such as Doriot, both Communists in their youth before turning Fascist. Mussolini attracted many intellectuals: already in 1929 Ezra Pound had left Paris for Rome, but by 1938, Hitler's politics had become the inspiration for Fascist sympathizers. The far-right attracted literary (and other) hysteria, of which the troublingly brilliant Céline was to be the best example in the Forties.

Continuous riots, crisis and fear of Fascism led to the establishment, in May 1936 of the Popular Front, a loose union of Communists, Socialists and Radicals thrown together by common fears and led by Léon Blum, a Jewish premier, something France had never known before. Whatever one's political beliefs had been before, they now turned into a cause worth defending. When, a couple of months later the Spanish Civil War began, the main question was whether or not to send troops to defend the only other Popular Front in Europe. The triumph of Franco over the legal

UNEMPLOYED protesting, 14 April 1935. Another of the almost daily demonstrations to protest against unemployment, here on the Left Bank. As the banners proclaim, the CGT, the Communist trade union, clamours for jobs instead of unemployment benefit. While the country's economy was being bungled, war was on its way as Hitler was busy re-arming.

government spelled doom to democracy, civil rights and freedom. In the same year, Hitler reoccupied the Rhineland. Just as France had not moved to defend Republican Spain, it remained aloof when Hitler marched into Austria in March 1938 and sought pointless compromise at the ignominious Munich conference in the autumn of that year. By then there were enough people around to make Fascism, for all its dreadfulness, totally plausible and indeed desirable.

Meantime, in the salon, all thought was tainted by the fashionable theories of the day, albeit watered down. Psychoanalysis and relativity, Freud and Einstein, soon to be declared degenerate by Nazi Germany, were dished out in sometimes incredible ways to explain the origins and implications of the crisis. For philosophers and a generally more cultivated public, a spate of translations of the Danish philosopher Kierkegaard sowed the seeds of Existentialism, to be developed to its full glory by Jean-Paul Sartre. Political literature suggested that it was possible through action to change one's personal fate and that of society, as André Malraux argued in novels such as *La Condition Humaine* (1933) and *L'Espoir* (1937), which takes place in the Spanish Civil War.

In fashion, the fuller figure was back, nursing curves were in as always happens when traditional family values come to the fore. Exit the sleek *garçonne*, re-enter neo-Victorian flounces, under-paid female labour complete with medals for the most prolific breeders, and soon the death penalty for abortionists. In France, save for some of the immigrants, the birth-rate was lower than the death-rate. With impending war, canon fodder was in urgent need.

This complicated era needs also to be understood in the context of pacifist passion which united those on both the Right and the Left against war. Scarred by the First World War, this was more than most people could face, even with a Fascist state active at almost every French border. The militantly pacifist novelist Jean Giono even went as far as stating in 1937 'What's the worst that can happen if Germany invades France? Become Germans? For my part, I prefer being a living German than a dead Frenchman'. On each political wing, there were thinkers primarily worried about anything within France that might draw their government into conflict with Germany. So both sides proceeded to blame Jews for causing agitation, and anti-Semitism was justified by allegations of the evil doings

CASINO DE PARIS, December 1939. A scene from the review *Paris London*, which ran from November 1939 to May 1940 and was designed to attract British soldiers on leave. The show included Josephine Baker and Maurice Chevalier.
(PHOTO: ISAAC KITROSSER)

of Jewish warmongering bankers eager to sell weapons and start the next war. Foreigners who had contributed to a degree of economic buoyancy in the Twenties were now perceived as undesirable and the source of all of France's problems.

When the Germans marched into Paris in 1940, not all the intellectuals fled. In fact, many stayed, grumbled certainly, but prospered. To talk of manipulation and ignorance of Nazi terror in order to excuse writers and artists is unfair: Céline and Drieu and, in wartime Paris, the likes of Cocteau, Arletty or Sacha Guitry were uncomfortably aware of their engagement to a by now totally acceptable and politically correct Fascist reality. With hindsight, France's capitulation to Germany could have been predicted. In many ways, the threshold of what was acceptable in terms of human rights and dignity had been sufficiently lowered as to make moral capitulation possible even before 1939. The City of Lights was on the wane, its marvellous creativity flickered, night and fog was about to shroud what had once been the capital of art and imagination.

STREET SCENE in the Marais district in 1931, with houses being demolished. Though the posters are for classic household goods they are in the most avant-garde graphic styles. Along the bottom are posters relaying a speech by President Doumergue at the end of his seven year term. These were printed by *L'Ami du Peuple*, a daily newspaper sponsored by the Fascist sympathiser François Coty, the perfume manufacturer, and sold at less than half the price of the other dailies.
(PHOTO: LOUIS CAILLAUD)

*W*AITERS on strike on 11 June 1936 (*above*). Despite the Popular Front being in power from May 1936, no less than 12,142 strikes, counted by the Minister of Labour, took place in the next month. Here the waiters have stormed out of the café-tabac with their trade union representative after having handed the patron their proposal for a collective contract in order to guarantee their precarious rights. All through the Thirties, waiters and hotel chamber-maids frequently went on strike.

*C*OLLECTING ingredients for a soup kitchen in Montmartre, 20 January 1935 (*opposite*). Charitable private initiatives of all kind flourished in the hungry Thirties, in lieu of an efficient social policy. Soup kitchens were prevalent, run either by the clergy, conscientious socialites or local town-halls. This collection, using a lorry, was organized by the Commune Libre du Vieux Montmartre. A kindly fishmonger displays her donation to the cause.

*T*HE INTERIOR of the Soviet Pavilion, 1937 International Exhibition. This, the first hall, pays tribute to Stalin's forced collectivization and industrialization by presenting idealized prowess in the field of industry (hence the motor car), natural resources and agriculture. As Yofan, the architect of the pavilion stated, the pavilion 'was designed as a triumphal building, reflecting in its dynamics...the enthusiasm and joy of this great age of ours, that of the building of Socialism, when work is a matter of honour, valour and heroism'. The 1937 Exhibition was full of such indicators of the political polarization that was to shatter the world order at the end of the decade
(PHOTO: THÉRÈSE BONNEY)

*P*ODIUM OF HONOUR in the German pavilion, 1937 International Exhibition. On the wall on the left is a Gobelins tapestry of Adolf Ziegler's triptych *The Four Elements*, the original of which hung in the Führerhaus in Munich. The pavilion was a monument to Nazi mythology, at once fortress, sarcophagus and church. It was meant to represent some kind of continuity with classical Rome and an ancient Germanic past. Here swastikas were present everywhere, on the façade mosaics, in the ironwork, on the stain-glass windows, an ominous prelude to those that were to invade so many of the countries present at the exhibition.

(PHOTO: THÉRÈSE BONNEY)

*L*ISTENING to the news of the Spanish Civil War, 12 August 1936. In a tiny café frequented by Catalans, *Ybghi*, Spanish expatriates listen to the latest news bulletin. In France, the main question was whether or not to send troops to defend the only other Popular Front in Europe. The triumph of Franco over the legal government spelled doom to democracy, civil rights and freedom, but France did not move, much to the horror of thinking intellectuals, many of whom enrolled in the International Brigades.

LISTENING to a broadcast by Hitler on 28 April 1939 (*above*). This restaurant offers the possibility for Fascist sympathisers to listen to Hitler whilst enjoying their lunch. By then, the German troups had marched into Czechoslovakia (15-16 March) whilst preparing to invade Poland. World War Two had all but begun.

MOBILISED artists' party, 31 October 1938 (*left*). In the inter-war years, fancy-dress parties were a weekly event in Montparnasse. This one is a more sinister affair, as the dress was military and the invitations were replicas of call-up papers.

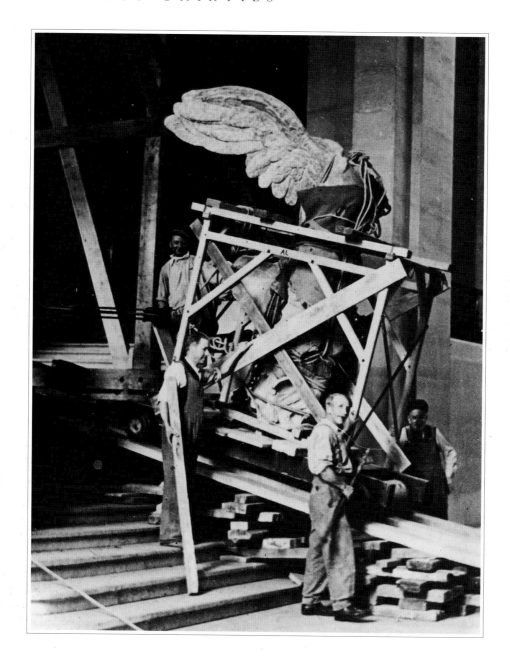

*P*REPARATIONS for war, September 1939 (*above*). Removal of the Victory of Samothrace from the Louvre. André Gide reflects the anguish of the age in his wartime diary (10 September 1939): 'We are all trying to protect our relics from destruction, no place is safe, a bomb can destroy an entire museum, each and every monument can be submerged by the flood of barbarity'. (PHOTO: NOËL LE BOYER)

*P*REPARATIONS for war, September 1939 (*opposite*). After Hitler's invasion of Poland, Britain, followed by France, declared war on Germany on 3 September 1939. Troops were deployed from the Ardennes to the North Sea and in Paris authorities started to protect national monuments from attack. Here sandbags are being placed against the cathedral of Notre Dame. The *drôle de guerre*, as this half-hearted war was called, was over in a few months and in June, Général Weygand declared Paris an open city and the Germans triumphantly marched in. (PHOTO: NOËL LE BOYER)

SUMMER 1940. Between 10 June and 14 June some two million Parisians, mainly old people, women and children fled Paris. As Gide recalls in his wartime diary 'The roads are filled with wandering families fleeing without knowing where they are going. Children have been lost and their desperate parents seek them'. In fact thousands of children were lost in the confusion. The near-senile Maréchal Pétain, now head of state, decided that this exodus justified France's capitulation to Nazi Germany. (PHOTO: NOËL LE BOYER)

BIBLIOGRAPHY

Jean-Paul Crespelle: *Montparnasse vivant*, Hachette, Paris, 1962

Jean-Paul Crespelle: *Montmartre vivant*, Hachette, Paris, 1964

William Rubin: *Dada and Surrealist Art*, Thames and Hudson, London, 1969

Maurice Nadeau: *The History of Surrealism*, Penguin, Harmondsworth, 1973

James R. Mellow: *Charmed Circle: Gertrude Stein and Company*, Avon Books, New York, 1974

Noel Riley Fitch: *Sylvia Beach and the Lost Generation: A History of Literary Paris in the Twenties and Thirties*, W.W. Norton, New York, 1983

Kenneth E. Silver and Romy Golan, eds: *The Circle of Montparnasse: Jewish Artists in Paris, 1905-45*, Universe, New York, 1985

Christopher Green: *Cubism and Its Enemies: Modern Movements and Reactions in French Art, 1916-28*, Yale University Press, New Haven and London, 1987

Douglas and Madeleine Johnson: *The Age of Illusion: Art and Politics in France, 1918-1940*, Thames and Hudson, London, 1987

Paris 1937: Cinquantenaire de l'Exposition des Arts et des Techniques dans la Vie Moderne, exhibition catalogue, Musée de l'art moderne de la ville de Paris, Paris, 1987

Martin Battersby and Philippe Garner: *The Decorative Twenties*, Whitney Library of Design, New York, 1988

Martin Battersby and Philippe Garner: *The Decorative Thirties*, Whitney Library of Design, New York, 1988

Billy Klüver and Julie Martin: *Kiki's Paris: Artists and Lovers, 1900-1930*, Abrams, New York, 1989

Kenneth E. Silver: *Esprit de Corps: The Art of the Parisian Avant-Garde and the First World War, 1914-1925*, Thames and Hudson, London, 1989

Helena Lewis: *Dada Turns Red: The Politics of Surrealism*, Edinburgh University Press, Edinburgh, 1990

Yvonne Brunhammer and Suzanne Tise: *The Decorative Arts in France: La Société des Artistes Décorateurs, 1900-1942*, Rizzoli, New York, 1991

George Melly: *Paris and the Surrealists*, photos by Michael Woods, Thames and Hudson, London, 1991

Nancy Troy: *Modernism and the Decorative Arts in France: Art Nouveau to Le Corbusier*, Yale University Press, New Haven and London, 1991

Victor Arwas: *Art Deco*, Academy Editions, London, 1992

Vincent Cronin: *Paris: City of Light, 1919-1939*, HarperCollins, London, 1994

Jean-Marie Drot: *Les Heures chaudes de Montparnasse*, Editions Hazan, Paris, 1995

Romy Golan: *Modernity and Nostalgia: Art and Politics in France between the Wars*, Yale University Press, New Haven and London, 1995

Eugen Weber: *The Hollow Years: France in the 1930s*, Sinclair Stevenson, London, 1995 (The author found this work especially useful.)

INDEX

PICTURE ACKNOWLEDGEMENTS

THE PUBLISHERS would particularly like to thank the following for their help in obtaining pictures: Liza Daum of the Bibliothèque Historique de la Ville de Paris, who made available the rich collections of that institution and without whose assistance this book would not have been possible; Thérèse Blondet-Bisch of the Bibliothèque Internationale Contemporaine, Paris, whose advice was invaluable at the early stages of photographic research; Thomas Gunther; Brad Newgent of the Cooper-Hewitt Museum, New York; Brigitte Vincens of the Centre de Documentation, Musée Nationale d'Art Moderne, Paris; and Ornella Volta at the Archives de la Fondation Erik Satie, Paris.

Bibliothèque de L'Arsenal, Paris: 89; 97 (Collection Jacques Copeau, cliché H. Manuel); 124

Bibliothèque Historique de la Ville de Paris: 11 (© Gaston Paris, courtesy BHVP); 16 (© Bonney/BHVP); 20 (© Bibliothèque Nationale de France, courtesy BHVP); 21 (© BHVP/Fonds France Soir); 24 above (© BHVP/Fonds France Soir); 26 above (© Bonney/BHVP); 36-37 (© Bonney/BHVP); 39 (© Bonney/BHVP); 41 (© Bonney/BHVP); 42-43 (© BHVP/Fonds France Soir); 51 (© Bonney/BHVP); 53 (© Bonney/BHVP); 58 below (© BHVP/Fonds France Soir); 60 (© Bibliothèque Nationale de France, courtesy BHVP); 61 (© Interpress, courtesy BHVP); 63 (© BHVP/Fonds France Soir); 64 (© Bonney/BHVP); 65 (© Zucca/BHVP); 88 (© Agence France Press, courtesy BHVP); 91 (© Bonney/BHVP); 98 (© Bonney/BHVP); 101 (© Bonney/BHVP); 105 (© Bonney/BHVP); 109 (© Agence France Press, courtesy BHVP); 112 (© Bonney/BHVP); 125 (© Bonney/BHVP); 128 (© Bonney/BHVP); 129 (© Bonney/BHVP); 133 (© Bonney/BHVP); 137 (© BHVP/Fonds France Soir); 144-5 (© Bonney/BHVP); 152 (© BHVP/Fonds France Soir); 155 (© Bonney/BHVP); 161 (© Bonney/BHVP); 162 (© Bonney/BHVP); 173 above (© BHVP); 176 (© Bonney/BHVP); 177 (© Bonney/BHVP); 180 (© Bonney/BHVP); 181 (© Bonney/BHVP); 185 below (© Bonney/BHVP); 186 (© Bibliothèque Nationale de France, courtesy BHVP); 190 (© BHVP/Fonds France Soir); 191 (© BHVP/Fonds France Soir); 192 (© BHVP/Fonds France Soir); 194 (© Isaac Kitrosser, courtesy BHVP); 196 (© Bibliothèque Nationale de France, courtesy BHVP); 197 (© Bibliothèque Nationale de France, courtesy BHVP); 198 (© Bonney/BHVP); 199 (© Bonney/BHVP); 200 (© Bibliothèque Nationale de France, courtesy BHVP); 201 below (© Interpress, courtesy BHVP); 201 above (© BHVP/Fonds France Soir)

Bibliothèque Nationale de France, Paris: 102, 103 (Cabinet des Estampes, Collection Delaunay); 58 above, 59, 66-67, 130, 131, 156, 172 above, 173 below (Cabinet des Estampes, Collection Meurisse)

Courtesy Kathleen Blumenfeld, Paris: 13

Courtesy Madame Marie-Jeanne Dinand-Caillaud: 28; 29; 195

Musée Carnavalet, Paris/© DACS 1996: 26 below; 46

Caisse Nationale des Monuments Historiques et des Sites, Paris/© DACS 1996: 10; 56-57; 68 both; 70-71; 74 above; 85; 116; 122; 123; 140; 142; 143; 146; 147; 148; 150; 153; 159; 160; 165; 167; 168 below; 170 both; 171; 172 below; 174-5; 178-9; 182-3

Cooper-Hewitt, National Design Museum, Smithsonian Institution/Art Resource New York: 52 both; 69 both; 72; 73; 74 below; 75; 117; 119; 120; 132; 139; 141; 149

Courtesy T Gunther, Paris: 44; 45; 100; 108; 110

La Mission du Patrimoine Photographique, Pars; Photo A. Kertész © Ministère de la Culture, France: 14; 27; 32; 34; 104-5

La Mission du Patrimoine Photographique, Paris; Photo E. Kollar © Ministère de la Culture, France: 135

La Mission du Patrimoine Photographic, Paris; © Association des Amis de Jacques-Henri Lartigue, Paris: 62; 134 below; 157; 166

Photo Musée des Arts Décoratifs, Paris: 184; 185 above; Photo Musée des Arts Décoratifs, Paris, Éditions A. Lévy, Paris: 164; 168 above © DACS 1996: 169

Musée d'Histoire Contemporaine-BDIC, Paris/photo Archipel: 6; 7; 8; 9; 12; 54; 55; 202; 203; 204

Musée Nationale d'Art Moderne, Centre de Documentation, Paris: 87; 106 below; 188; 106 above, 107 (Collection Bibliothèque Littéraire Jacques Doucet, Paris, courtesy MNAM)

Musée National d'Art Moderne, Centre Georges Pompidou, Paris: 35, 99, 115 (Gift of Madame Renée Beslon, 1982); 111 (© Man Ray Trust/ADAGP, Paris and DACS, London 1996)

Robert Harding Picture Library, London; 30-31

© Roger-Viollet, Paris: 25; 38; 127; 163 (© Branger-Viollet); 17 (© Martinie-Viollet) © Harlingue-Viollet: 22-23; 33; 48; 79; 18; 40; 49; 83; 86; 96; 126; 134 above

Archives de la Fondation Erik Satie, Paris: 24 below; 78 (© Man Ray Trust/ADAGP, Paris and DACS, London 1996); 82; 92 both; 93; 94 both; 95 both

Courtesy Sotheby's, London; 76; 136

Courtesy the Trustees of the Victoria & Albert Museum, London: 81 (Theatre Museum)